Daily Prayer

in the

Reformed Tradition:

An Initial Survey

by Diane Karay Tripp
Minister of the Presbyterian Church (U.S.A.)

THE ALCUIN CLUB and the GROUP FOR RENEWAL OF WORSHIP (GROW)
The Alcuin Club, which exists to promote the study of Christian liturgy in general and of Anglican liturgy in particular, traditionally published a single volume annually for its members. This ceased in 1986 but resumed in 1992. Similarly, GROW was responsible from 1975 to 1986 for the quarterly 'Grove Liturgical Studies'. Since the beginning of 1987 the two have sponsored a Joint Editorial Board to produce 'Joint Liturgical Studies', of which the present Study is no. 35. There are lists on pages 44-46 in this Study, and further details are available from the address below. Both also produce separate publications.

THE COVER PICTURE
is a copyright design by Susan Ball Lehman

First Impression September 1996
ISSN 0951-2667
ISBN 1 85174 324 3

GROVE BOOKS LIMITED
RIDLEY HALL RD CAMBRIDGE CB3 9HU

CONTENTS

Diane Karay Tripp is a minister of the Presbyterian Church (U.S.A.) and earned the M.A. in Liturgical Studies from the University of Notre Dame. She served as an editorial consultant for the *Book of Common Worship* (1993) and is the author of several articles on liturgical subjects.

This is a revised version of two articles that originally appeared in *Studia Liturgica 21* (1991) pp.76-107 and 190-219. Informed by five years of further research, this Study paints a bolder picture. New topics explored are the role of thanksgiving in Reformed devotion, exposition in family worship, and public and family prayer in mission settings such as Hawaii, Africa and Vanuatu. Attention is given to African slaves in America as well as to Puritan Native Americans.

Introduction

The churches of the Reformed tradition have, from their beginning, observed daily prayer in church and home, offering the sacrifice of praise to God the Father through Jesus Christ in the Holy Spirit, in obedience to the apostolic injunction, 'pray without ceasing.' In the communities of public assembly, family, husband and wife, and the individual in God's presence, they have prayed as members of the body of Christ.

The Reformers and later Reformed ministers scrutinized their late medieval inheritance (already undergoing change), criticizing and reforming many practices. Concerns were for active, spiritual worship as opposed to rote or mechanical devotion, intelligibility (beginning with the use of the vernacular), accessibility by all to the means of grace, and insistence on integrity and ethical conduct, with special concern for charity, both in affection and deed, for the needy, sick and poor, the face of Christ visible in one's suffering neighbour.[1]

At the same time, much medieval devotional practice was continued with little if any change, in such areas as fasting, meditation, the gestures of reverence, and devotional readings and prayers.[2]

The Reformed sought a return to Christian origins through reference to the life of the primitive and early church. Countless treatises and prayer manuals document biblical and patristic precedent for virtually every aspect of religious life.[3]

Paul Bradshaw has suggested that the daily prayer of the ordinary folk of Reformation traditions might prove to be a fruitful research field. This study, now revised, is one response, and seeks to provide both a foundation and framework for further studies.[4]

I survey Reformed daily prayer in its public and domestic communities from the sixteenth through the nineteenth centuries, with brief reference to the twentieth century. First, however, let us examine the core of Reformed spirituality: the spiritual sacrifice of God's covenant people, the church.

---

[1] J. K. S. Reid, trans., *Calvin: Theological Treatises*, Library of Christian Classics 22 (SCM, London, 1954) 1536 Genevan Confession, p.29; *Genuine Works of Robt. Leighton*, new ed (London, 1812) vol. 3 p.250; *Sermons of Iohn Calvin, vpon the Booke of Iob*, tr A Golding (London, 1574) p.4; J. F. Ostervald, *The Grounds and Principles of the Christian Religion*, tr H. Wanley, revised by G. Stanhope, 7th ed (London, 1765) pp.211-259; Elsie Ann McKee, *John Calvin on the Diaconate and Liturgical Almsgiving* (Librairie Droz, Genève. 1984).

[2] *The Oxford Encyclopedia of the Reformation* sv 'Piety, ' by Maureen Flynn, 3: 266; Tessa Watt, *Cheap Print and Popular Piety, 1550-1640* (Cambridge Univsity Press, Cambridge, 1991) pp.126, 328; Richard P. Gildrie, *The Profane, the Civil & The Godly: The Reformation of Manners in Orthodox New England, 1679-1740* (Pennsylvania State University Press, University Park, PA, 1994) p.111; G. W. Sprott, ed *The Book of Common Order of the Church of Scotland* (Edinburgh, 1901) pp.208-210, note p.210, no. 5 for a possible medieval source of Calvin's evening prayer.

[3] Theodore Dwight Bozeman, *To Live Ancient Lives: The Primitivist Dimension in Puritanism* (University of North Carolina Press, Chapel Hill, 1988) pp.13-50; the Old or First Testament was cited by the Reformed as often as Christian scripture.

[4] Paul F. Bradshaw, 'Whatever Happened to Daily Prayer?' in *Worship* 64 (1990) p.19. See the ff for background: Charles E. Hambrick-Stowe, *The Practice of Piety: Devotional Disciplines in Seventeenth-Century New England* (University of North Carolina Press, Chapel Hill, 1982); E. B. Holifield, *The Covenant Sealed: The Development of Puritan Sacramental Theology in Old and New England, 1570-1720* (Yale University Press, New Haven, 1974); J. Morgan, *Godly Learning: Puritan Attitudes towards Reason, Learning, and Education, 1560-1640* (Cambridge University Press, Cambridge, 1986); Gordon S. Wakefield, *Puritan Devotion: Its Place in the Development of Christian Piety* (Epworth, London, 1957); Helen C. White, *English Devotional Literature (Prose) 1600-1640* (University of Wisconsin Press, Madison, 1931; reprint ed, Haskell House, NY, 1966); *idem, The Tudor Books of Private Devotion* (University of Wisconsin Press, Madison, 1951; reprint ed, Greenwood Press, Westport, Conn, 1979); Leigh Eric Schmidt, *Holy Fairs: Scottish Communions and American Revivals in the Early Modern Period* (Princeton University Press, Princeton, 1989); Kenneth Boyd, *Scottish Church Attitudes to Sex, Marriage and the Family, 1850-1914* (John Donald, Edinburgh, 1980) ch 5; Colleen McDannel, *The Christian Home in Victorian America, 1840-1900* (Indiana University Press, Bloomington, 1986); *The Oxford Encyclopedia of the Reformation*, 4 vols, 1996, offers uneven treatment of relevant topics.

1. The Church, 'All one Body'

Reformed folk prayed as members of the whole people of God, whether in solitude, with spouse, family, or in public assembly. The opening words of the Lord's Prayer witnessed to the corporate character of all prayer. Note Théodore de Bèze's paraphrase on the *incipit:* 'Thus every faithful creature sayeth unto thee, Our Father, give unto us, forgive us. For thus hath thy Son, the head of that union which is among all Christians, commanded, that our prayers should be common for all thy people, as being all one body, which thou governest by one only Spirit . . .'[1] William Gouge freely quotes from Cyprian's *De Oratione Dominica* (Ch ii), 'we pray not for one, but for the whole church, because we are all one.' His son Thomas read Acts 12.12 as teaching that 'joint prayers are better than the prayers of the same persons apart.'[2]

The dominant image of family religion, 'church in the house,' reflects the unity of public and domestic worship.[3] The domestic church included worship, instruction, governance, discipline, and the exercise of charity and justice; it supported the gathered church and was its refuge in time of persecution.[4] For besieged Puritans and Huguenots, the image recalled apostolic gatherings for worship as well as the secretive assemblies of primitive Christians.

In addition, the ecclesial character of Reformed daily prayer is seen in individual and family use of prayers from public liturgy wherever such liturgy existed, and in individual and family preparation for the Lord's Day and the sacrament of the Lord's Supper.[5]

1. WOMEN

An holistic understanding of Christ's body is evident in the writings of sixteenth- and seventeenth-century Reformed writers. They understood that Christ's humanity, not his maleness, was salvific: women, as well as men, reflect the *Imago Dei.* Calvin is explicit that both men and women are created in God's image.[6] English Puritan sermons and counsel use relatively inclusive language, recall biblical women, and employ metaphors for the divine life that embrace male and female. Sometimes a Puritan adapts scripture so as to make it more inclusive.

The English Puritan divine Henry Smith (1550?-1591) exemplifies most of the above points. His sermons circulated throughout the country and were widely used by families

---

[1] *Maister Bezaes Hovshold Prayers* [tr John Barnes] (London, 1603) 1st pr. This present study modernizes spelling and punctuation.

[2] William Gouge, *A Gvide to Goe to God*, 2nd ed (London, 1636) p.21; Thomas Gouge, *A Word to Sinners, And a Word to Saints* (London, 1673) p.232.

[3] See, for example, John Leland, *Forms of Devotion* (London, 1766) pp.xviii-xix.

[4] Job Orton, *Religious Exercises recommended* (Shrewsbury,1769) pp.60, 102.

[5] Huguenot leader Coligny used French Reformed liturgy for family prayer. See C. W. Baird, *The Presbyterian Liturgies* [1st ed as *Eutaxia*, 1855] (reprint, Baker, Grand Rapids, 1960) p.80. J. C. Werndly remarks on the value of the set prayers of the Zurich liturgy: 'For ignorant people, when they hear set forms repeated, will at last get them by heart, and so be enabled to pray both at home and church,' *Liturgia Tigurina* (London, 1693) sigs A6ʳ⁻ᵛ.

[6] *The Sermons of M. Iohn Calvin Vpon the Fifth Booke of Moses called Deuteronomie . . .*, tr A. Golding [1583], 16th-17th Century Facsimile Eds (Banner of Truth Trust, Oxford and Carlisle, PA, 1987) p.210.

in household worship. Other early Reformed writers whose language is carefully inclusive, and whose works enjoyed wide circulation are John Bradford, Edward Dering, William Bridge, and Richard Alleine. French Reformed pastor Charles Drelincourt (1595-1669) addresses both sexes: 'Take good courage, my brother, or my sister, and be not frightened at the sight of death.'[1]

How was this understanding of the Body reflected in practice? Puritan domestic manuals generally required submissiveness in the marital relationship. But women were expected to counsel their children; marriage was not simply for procreation and the avoidance of fornication, but also for mutual comfort and spiritual companionship.[2] Women were viewed with sufficient seriousness to be the subject of biographies.

Increasing respect for women elevated their position from a traditional role as spiritual guide for daughters to deputy household priest. Perkins apart, 'Writer after writer insists that wherever a husband shows himself unfitted for this task, whether spiritually or physically, the wife should replace him.'[3]

William Gouge states that the husband is the wife's 'mouth to God,' under ordinary circumstances, but conceded that many women were better at prayer, and should be allowed to pray aloud.[4] Among women who led family worship in their husbands' absence were Eleanor Penry, wife of Welsh Puritan martyr John Penry (1563?-1593) and Ann Hulton (1668-1697) sister of Matthew Henry. All of Philip Henry's daughters were taught to write sermons and used them in daily family worship in their married households.[5] A century later, Independent minister Job Orton portrayed wives as obliged to encourage their husbands in 'family duty,' and if they refused, the duty devolved to them. Furthermore, husbands should provide their spouses with prayer 'forms' that the daily sacrifice might not cease in their absence. Women also served as deputy priests in North America from colonial times through the nineteenth century.[6] This practice did not uniformly survive into the twentieth century.

In addition to leading family worship, at least on an occasional basis, women sometimes wrote down their prayers. Those of Elizabeth Singer Rowe (1674-1737) were published; many more are found in diaries.[7]

---

[1] *The Works of Henry Smith* (Edinburgh, 1866-7) see vol 1, pp.122-3, vol 2: pp.85, 164-5, 205, 299; Charles Drelincourt, *The Christian's Defence Against the Fears of Death*, tr M. D'Assigny, new ed (London, 1814) p.234.

[2] Morgan, *op. cit.*, p.143. See P. Collinson, *The Elizabethan Puritan Movement* (Jonathan Cape, London, 1967) p.93 for an indication of women's public role.

[3] L. L. Schücking, *The Puritan Family*, tr B. Battershaw (Routledge & Kegan Paul, London, 1969) p.40. From at least Puritan times, women typically taught children to pray. James Janeway's *Token for Children* (London, 1676), one of the most widely read books among Puritans, assumes this to be standard. sig A9^r.

+W. Gouge, *Of Domesticall Duties*, 3rd ed (London, 1634) p.237.

[5] William Pierce, *John Penry* (London, 1923) p.406. John B. Williams, *The Henry Family Memorialized* (London, [1840]) pp.83, 118-9.

[6] Orton, *op. cit.*, p.148; McDannell, *op. cit.*, p.112. American Presbyterian minister Ashbel Green (1762-1848) recorded that his mother always prayed with the family when her husband was absent: *Life of Ashbel Green* (NY, 1849) p.19.

[7] I. Watts, ed, *Devout Exercises of the Heart. . . . by Mrs. Elizabeth Rowe* (Alcester 1814). Of special note: Samuel Hopkins, *Memoirs of the Life of Mrs. Sarah Osborn* (Worcester, Mass, 1799). On women who made piety a career, see Sara Heller Mendelson, *The Mental World of Stuart Women: Three Studies* (University of Massachusetts Press, Amherst, 1987) p.9.

2. CHILDREN

Children were integral members of God's people. Puritan parents began religious instruction of their children as early as possible. Before William and Elizabeth Gouge's children were three years old, they could answer simple catechism questions.[1] The *First Book of Discipline* (1560) of the Scottish church required the ability to recite the Lord's Prayer, the Belief, and Ten Commandments before admittance to the Lord's Table. Similar knowledge was required of children in late seventeenth-century New England.[2] Rudolf Boon has shown that children in eighteenth-century Netherlands inhabited the same world as adults. Among intellectual families it was not uncommon for four-year-olds to read and write, and for twelve-year-olds to have mastered French, Latin and Greek. Dutch children's attainments in the sixteenth and seventeenth centuries were similar.[3]

Janeway's *Token for Children* portrays several children showing the signs of salvation and fervent piety from the age of two or three. This sounds unlikely to us, but did occur in an era that expected, 'when we cannot run to Christ, we should creep unto him, and serve him as we can in youth and age.' Even children's play reflected the centrality of religion: accounts of nursery preachers are numerous, and even in this century children 'played church.'[4] There are also accounts of children leading family worship.[5] Children were sometimes furnished with prayers suitable to their development.[6] Beginning in the eighteenth century we find prayerbooks for children and youth.

3. SERVANTS AND SLAVES

Servants were viewed as family members and expected to attend public and family worship, and to pray privately. Puritans expected servants and apprentices to read the Bible with special attention to 'the precepts, promises, threatenings, and examples' regarding servants. They were to labour faithfully, without murmuring, to look to God for their chief reward; to submit to the governance of master and mistress, and to pray for their work and the family. Masters, likewise, had responsibilities: to remember that their servants were fellow servants of Christ who must be ruled with love, preserved from injury, and provided good food, lodging and wages.[7]

---

[1] Schücking, *op. cit.*, p.68; Nicholas Guy, *Pieties Pillar. Or, A Sermon Preached at the Funerall of Mistresse Elizabeth Gouge* (London, 1626) p.46.

[2] G. B. Burnet, *The Holy Communion in the Reformed Church of Scotland, 1560-1960* (Oliver and Boyd, Edinburgh, 1960) p.45. See also C. Mather, *Small Offers Towards the Service of the Tabernacle in the Wilderness* (Boston, 1689) p.46. Hughes Oliphant Old, *The Shaping of the Reformed Baptismal Rite in the Sixteenth Century*, (Wm B Eerdmans, Grand Rapids, 1992) pp.179-200 on catechetical instruction.

[3] R. Boon, 'Child and Church, Communion and culture' in *Omnes Circumadstantes: Contributions toward a history of the role of people in the liturgy*, ed C. Caspers and M. Schneiders (Kok, Kampen, 1990) pp.222-4.

[4] Janeway, *op. cit.*, pp.19-21; *Works of Henry Smith*, vol 2, p.84; Schücking, *op. cit.*, p.69; R. [Cowell], *Memorials of a Gracious Life with the Diary and Letters of George Cowell* (London, 1895) p.4. Personal communication with Luella Karay (1990) raised in the Reformed Church in America.

[5] Orton, *op. cit.*, p.149; Edward T. Corwin, *A Manual of the Reformed Church in America*, 2nd ed (NY, 1869) pp.102-3, 105.

[6] Richard Baxter, *Practical Works* (London, 1707), 'Poor Mans Family Book' in vol 4, pp.249-50.

[7] Abraham Jackson, *The Pious Prentice* (London, 1640) pp.4-5. Baxter, 'Christian Directory' [CD] henceforth with reference to vol 1, *Practical Works*, 1707 ed; II, 13, pp.435-7; II, 14, pp.437ff. The Puritan Countess of Warwick, Mary Boyle Rich (1625-78) was exemplary in spiritual care for her servants: D. Dana, ed *Memoirs of Eminently Pious Women*, abridged from Gibbon's London ed (Newburyport, 1803) p.112.

Faith in the inclusivity of Christ's Body was severely tested by slavery. Cotton Mather's views illustrate the conflict of godly people with an ungodly institution. Mather owned a slave and was indignant when a military officer named his own slave, 'Cotton Mather.' Yet Mather was concerned for slaves' welfare and operated a school to instruct them in reading and religion, at his own expense. He admonished others that Africans were one's neighbour and advocated their evangelization and baptism, yet reassured slave-owners that baptism granted only heavenly, not earthly, liberty. Similarly, Dutch Reformed South African colonists educated and baptized slave children, yet listed their names on a separate register, implying that they were not fully or really Christian.[1]

Christianity was a major factor in mitigating cruel treatment by masters. Ministers reminded masters of biblical obligations to slaves, and pointed to the 'one Master in heaven', both of slave and free (Ephesians 6.9). Presbyterian minister James Thornwell preached that Africans and whites were both created in God's image. However this truth was viewed, thousands of slaves were exposed to Christianity. For various reasons, more settled in Baptist and Methodist than in Reformed church traditions.[2]

---

[1] W. C. Ford, ed, *Diary of Cotton Mather*, Massachusetts Historical Society Collections, 7th Series, vol 8 (Boston, 1912). [Cotton Mather] *The Negro Christianized* (Boston, 1706) pp.5, 19, 25-6. Sondra A. O'Neale, *Jupiter Hammon and the Beginnings of African-American Literature* (American Theological Library Assc and The Scarecrow Press, Metuchen, NJ, 1993) pp.26-7. Jonathan N. Gerstner, *The Thousand Generation Covenant: Dutch Reformed Covenant Theology and Group Identity in Colonial South Africa, 1652-1814* (Brill, Leiden, 1991) p.249.

[2] John W. Blassingame, *The Slave Community: Plantation Life in the Antebellum South*, rev ed (Oxford University Press, NY and Oxford, 1979) pp.268-9.

2. A Living Sacrifice, 'in Gratitude Bound'

> Were the whole realm of nature mine,
> That were a present far too small;
> Love so amazing, so divine,
> Demands my soul, my life, my all.[1]

This stanza from the communion hymn of Congregational minister Isaac Watts (1674-1748) draws its imagery from traditional Reformed piety understood as sacrifice. This emphasis permeated every aspect of prayer life. It was at the core of the baptismal piety that flourished in the seventeenth and eighteenth centuries in Great Britain and New England, and, because the Lord's Supper was the primary occasion for covenant renewal, was at the centre of Reformed eucharistic piety as well.[2]

Prayer, as sacrifice, is a thankful response to the grace of God for self-giving to the point of death in Jesus Christ's crucifixion, and through his complete sacrifice, obtaining forgiveness and eternal life for unworthy creatures. Only a like sacrificial love is the proper response to this divine gift.[3] The scriptural basis is Pauline: 'I appeal to you therefore, brethren, by the mercies of God, to present your bodies as a living sacrifice, holy and acceptable to God, which is your spiritual worship' (Romans 12.1). This text underlies every aspect of devotional practice and occurs repeatedly in prayers, sermons and counsel. For example, English Presbyterian Henry Grove (1684-1738) includes these sentences in a prayer for use 'At the Lord's Table':

> Thou hast bought me with a price, even with the precious blood of thy own Son, of which this sacramental wine is a memorial. I therefore, as in gratitude bound, present my whole self, body and soul, to thee, a living sacrifice, holy and acceptable, which is my reasonable service, with a full purpose of heart to glorify thee with both.[4]

The Reformed understanding of prayer was in accord with patristic thought, such as the third-century Christians who 'viewed their acts of prayer as the true fulfillment of the "perpetual" sacrifices of the Old Testament.' John Preston, for example, stated that we should pray at least twice a day, citing the morning and evening sacrifices in the Temple. Presbyterian Benjamin Bennet (1674-1726) also noted the daily sacrifices under the law as one basis for twice-daily prayer, also adducing the 'continual sacrifice' (Num. 28.23-4) as warrant for praying without ceasing.[5] Théodore de Bèze urged:

---

[1] I. Watts, *The Psalms of David* [1st 1710] bound with *Hymns and Spiritual Songs* (London, 1815) Book III, 'Prepared for the Lord's Supper,' Hymn 7, v 5, p.186.

[2] [Cotton Mather], *Baptismal Piety. Two Brief Essays* (Boston, 1727).

[3] See John Howe, 'The Living Temple: A Treatise on Self-Dedication' in J. Wesley, ed, *A Christian Library* (Bristol, 1755) vol 48, pp.305-34.

[4] With Paul, 'body' is understood as the entire self. Henry Grove, *A Discourse Concerning the Nature and Design of the Lord's Supper*, 5th ed (London, 1742) p.56; I. Watts, in 'Guide to Prayer' included 'profession or self-dedication', rooted in the baptismal covenant as an essential aspect of all prayer. See *The Works of the Late and Reverend Isaac Watts, D.D.*, ed Jennings and Doddridge, (London, 1753) vol 3, pp.118-20 [Hereafter cited from this edn as GP].

[5] Paul F Bradshaw, 'Cathedral vs. Monastery: The only Alternatives for the Liturgy of the Hours?' in J. N. Alexander, ed, *Time and Community*, (Pastoral Press, Wash, DC, 1990) p.125; J. Preston, *The Saints Daily Exercise*, 5th ed (London, 1630) p.16; B. Bennet, *The Christian Oratory*, 6th ed (London, 1760) pp.642-3.

Let us pray and meditate, if not incessantly, yet at the least, daily at certain set hours, and as often as we may, as well in the congregation, as in our families, morning and evening, among our household, as also in our secret chambers. Thus shall we with our lips, upon the altars of our hearts, offer up many acceptable sacrifices of sweet savour before his presence. . . .[1]

Similar language recurs in Puritan and later Reformed writings, and the whole range of sacrificial imagery is used. Note the scripture passages appealed to by Reformed authors across several centuries: in response to the apostolic injunction 'pray without ceasing,' (I Thess. 5.17), people offered the morning and evening sacrifice (Ex. 29.39) or the continual burnt-offering (Lev. 6.12-13) from the altar of the contrite heart. Prayers ascended to God as incense (Ps. 141.2; Rev. 8.3-4), and the faithful waited for God, through the Holy Spirit, to cast down fire from heaven, consuming, and thus, accepting the gift (Lev. 9.24). The fire was felt in the heart as a burning (Ps. 39.3; Luke 24.32). When the heart is dry, advised Watts, tell God that without the Spirit, 'he must lose a morning or evening sacrifice if he condescend not to send down fire from heaven upon the altar.'[2]

The sacrificial heart of Reformed prayer declined severely throughout the nineteenth century. Prayer was more likely to be viewed as a means to moralistic or didactic ends than the living sacrifice required as holy service. In the late twentieth century this aspect of Reformed spirituality is neglected[3] and theologically suspect to many.

Renewal of the baptismal covenant is the most striking expression of Reformed sacrificial spirituality. Families were expected to instruct children about the meaning of baptism, leading them to a free and joyful consent, upon their admittance to the Lord's Supper, to the vows made in baptism, surrendering themselves wholly to God's will and service. Relinquishing everything to God, in return, they received union with Christ, and through him were made heirs of the world.[4]

Once made, the covenant could not be renewed too often. One Dutch pastor advised renewing one's covenant at least daily, on all prayer and fast days, whenever God's grace shone brightly on the soul, or one was faced with adversity. The Reformed focused on each participation in the Lord's Supper as an occasion for covenant renewal, as well as one's birthday and the New Year; it was also at the heart of 'secret' fast and thanksgiving days.[5]

Joseph Alleine and Philip Doddridge wrote instructions for making and renewing solemn covenants with God. Their books, Reformed spiritual classics, guided generations of

---

[1] *Maister Beza's Hovshold Prayers* (London, 1607 ed) sigs B11ᵛ-B12ʳ.
[2] Watts, GP, 133. See also F. Rous, *Oile of Scorpions* (London, 1623) p.300; W. Gouge, 'Epistle to the Reader' in R. Bolton, *Certain Devout Prayers upon Solemn Occasions* (London, 1638) sigs A6ᵛ-A7ʳ; Drelincourt, *op. cit.*, pp.140, 146, 150, 156-7, 361-2; Grove, *op. cit.*, pp.142-3, 145.
[3] For example, Howard L. Rice, *Reformed Spirituality: An Introduction for Believers* (Westminster/John Knox, Louisville, 1991): no explicit mention of sacrificial or covenant renewal spirituality.
[4] See, for example: Baxter, CD, II, 10, p.427; Matthew Henry, *An Account of the Life and Death of Mr. Philip Henry*, 4th ed (London, 1765) pp.101-4; O[liver] H[eywood] *Advice to an Only Child* (London, 1693) pp.4-10.
[5] Petrus Immens [1664-1720], *The Pious Communicant Encouraged* [ET of *De godvruchtige avondmaalganger*. . . ., Amsterdam 1758 ed] (NY, 2 vols, 1801-2) vol 2, pp.20-22.

Reformed faithful as well as Christians of other denominations.[1] The covenant was best committed to paper (generally in prayer form), signed, dated, and regularly reviewed, so that, finally internalized, the self-dedication could function as the 'soul's anchor', and a source of spiritual strength.[2]

Baptismal piety flourished in New England from the late 1670's onward. Holifield observes,

> 'Preachers recalled baptismal promises and congregations covenanted to observe baptismal vows. It was as if a host of zealous Puritans had suddenly discovered the usefulness of the visible rites and tangible sacraments that so frequently had aroused their suspicions.'[3]

Eventually, however, covenant renewal among the Reformed faded away, being all but dead by the mid-nineteenth century.

---

[1] J. Allein[e], 'An Alarm to Unconverted Sinners' in J Wesley, ed *A Christian Library* (London, 1822 ed) vol 14, pp.141-4; P Doddridge, *The Rise and Progress of Religion in the Soul*, 2nd ed (London, 1854) pp.159-68. Alleine's work was especially influential.

[2] See Watts, ed, *Devout Exercises*, pp.90-2; O. H[eywood] *Baptismal Bonds Renewed* (London, 1687); *The Power of Faith: Exemplified in the Life and Writings of the Late Mrs. Isabella Graham of New-York* (NY, printed; London, reprinted, 1816).

[3] Holifield, *op. cit.*, p.169; see also pp.169-96. Cf Hambrick-Stowe, *op. cit.*, pp.126-32 regarding church covenants.

3. Embodied Reverence:
'The Due Expression of the Heart'

Reformed Christians inherited the gestures and postures of reverence from the medieval church; ceremonial in public service was drastically pruned but not abolished.[1] Paul's appeal, 'present your bodies as a living sacrifice', provided one important warrant for embodied prayer. For Calvin, 'bodily exercises', though secondary to inward piety, were nonetheless an 'ordinary portion of Christian holiness,' and not the preserve of ascetics. In part, polemic motivated the emphasis on attentiveness and fervency in prayer. Calvin accused Catholics of severing outward devotional acts from feeling and deemed this a sacrilege.[2]

Ardor characterized Reformed devotional expression.[3] All prayer was viewed as being through the Holy Spirit, but ardor was a special sign of the Spirit's presence.[4] But devotion was not simply emotion.[5] When prayer was barren of feeling, Reformed folk knew that God was weaning the soul in order to fasten it solely on the divine will.[6]

Classical Reformed piety could not conceive of disembodied reverence of God. 'Your hearts must be first looked to, ' wrote Baxter, 'but your words and bodies must be next looked to. And if you regard not these, it is hardly credible that you regard your hearts. Your words and gestures are the due expression of your hearts.'[7]

Among the most important scriptural warrants for ritual expressiveness was Jesus' picture of the Publican (Luke 18.23), a potent image, reflecting devotional practice and providing a model of authentic humility before God. Thomas Collin's poem, *The Penitent Publican*, begins:

> On bended knees, and with a broken heart,
> Eyes cast on earth, hands beating of my breast;
> I come to act a penitential part,
> Before th'almighty who is pleasèd best
> With sinful souls, when they are thus addressed:
> In whose dread presence, caitiff that I am,
> Preparèd thus, till now, I never came.

---

[1] Diane Karay Tripp, 'The Reformed Tradition of Embodied Prayer' in *Liturgy* 8 (Summer 1990) pp.92-3.

[2] J. Calvin, *Commentary on the Epistles to Timothy, Titus and Philemon*, tr W. Pringle (Edinburgh, 1856) pp.109-10; J. Calvin, *Commentary on the Book of Psalms*, tr J. Anderson (Edinburgh, 1846) vol 2, p.275. Drelincourt: 'A groan of an oppressed soul, and a sigh from us by necessity, and a tear dropped from a penitent heart, are far more acceptable to him, than prayers of forty hours . . .' *op. cit.*, p.242.

[3] W. Gouge, *The Saints Sacrifice* (London, 1632) p.48.

[4] For example, J. Calvin, *Commentary upon the Epistle of Saint Paul to the Romans*, ed from ET of C. Rosdell by H. Beveridge (Edinburgh, 1844) p.224.

[5] H. Grove, *A Discourse of Secret Prayer* (London 1723) p.109.

[6] *M. Derings Workes* (London, 1597) sigs H2v-H3r.

[7] Baxter, CD, III.1, p.550. Also note: Susanne Woods, 'The Body Penitent: A 1560 Calvinist Sonnet Sequence' in *American Notes & Queries* 5 (1992) pp.137-40.

Knees ever bow, and standing bear no more,
Eyes ever weep, and ne'er be dry again;
Hands beat my breast, and make it ever sore,
Heart never cease, but sigh and sob amain:
Tongue, ever pray, and for my sins complain.
Till tears, blows, sighs, sobs, prayers, and complaints,
Have freed my soul from all her foul attaints.[1]

Each image corresponds to practice. Praying aloud, customary into the nineteenth century, was an aid against distraction and a catalyst to ardor. Isaac Watts notes that in the psalms David frequently cried aloud to God. Reformed praying was demonstrative, calling on God with sighs, groans and sobs. The most common warrant for weeping was Ps 6.6, 'I fainted in my mourning: I cause my bed every night to swim, and water my couch with tears' (Geneva Bible). Calvin declared that there was nothing extravagant here to those afflicted by terrors of conscience.[2] Cleansing tears washed penitents of corruption. American Presbyterian novelist Mary Terhune (b. 1831?) remarked that 'tears were fashionable' in the 1830's, and the 'subject of religion brought tears as naturally as the wringing of a moist sponge, water.'[3]

Kneeling was universal for family prayer into the nineteenth century, and the most frequent posture for private devotion. Hands were either held palms together, or slightly raised and spread towards heaven—a modified *orans* position.[4] Some, when renewing their baptismal covenant, raised up one hand to witness to the irrevocable nature of their contract with God.[5] When praying, eyes gazed either to heaven in confidence, or towards earth in penitence or dejection.[6]

Beating the breast during prayer of confession was not uncommon.[7] In the seclusion of one's chamber, prostration expressed a deep sense of sin, or was used by those who threw themselves, body and soul, before God's throne.[8]

Such demonstrative devotion was not without its in-house critics. Puritan writer John Norden discloses his bias: 'Lord, I know that thou hearest the very silent sighs and groans of the faithful heart.'[9] However, those who preferred subdued reverence appear to have been a quiet minority. Reformed folk did not want to be 'mere statues and lifeless engines of prayer.'[10]

---

[1] (London, 1610) sig B^r. Sole known copy: British Library, Shelfmark Huth 88. The poem is dedicated to Lady Katherine Hastings, Countess of Huntingdon.
[2] Watts, GP, p.140; Calvin, *Psalms*, vol 1 (1845) pp.72-3. Jesus' example and Ps. 126.5-6 were other warrants.
[3] [Mary Terhune] *Marion Harland's Autobiography* (New York, 1910) p.87.
[4] Karay Tripp, *op. cit.*, p.95. Common warrants for the latter were Ezra 9.5 and 2 Chron. 6.13.
[5] Immens, *op. cit.*, vol 2, p.15, citing Isa. 44.5. J. H. Turner, *The Rev. Oliver Heywood, B.A., 1630-1702* (Brighouse and Bingley, 1882-5) vol 1, p.309.
[6] Watts, GP, p.153.
[7] Doddridge, *op. cit.*, p.163. Karay Tripp, *op. cit.*, pp.95 and 97, note 22.
[8] Watts, GP, p.152. Gen. 17.3, Josh. 5.14 and Matt. 26.39 were common warrants. George W. Bethune, *Memoirs of Mrs. Joanna Bethune* (NY, 1863) p.63.
[9] J. Norden, *The Imitation of David* (London, 1624) p.183.
[10] Watts, GP, p.156.

2. PUBLIC WORSHIP

In public worship the Reformed have observed gestures of reverence from the earliest times.[1] Calvin viewed uncovering the head, kneeling and stretching forth the hands as conducive to reverence. Later generations also esteemed these gestures. Following the 'Rule of St Paul,' I Cor. 11.4-7, women covered their heads, while men uncovered theirs.[2] Anglican bishop Gilbert Burnet (1643-1715) felt this was nowhere better observed than in Basel, Switzerland where married women attended church wearing a 'coif' on their heads, so folded that it 'cometh down so far as to cover their eyes, so another fold covered also their mouth and chin, so that nothing but their nose appears; and then all turns backward in a folding that hangeth down to their mid-leg: this is always white. . . .'[3] Paul's 'Rule' was observed into the nineteenth century.

John Durel (1625-1683), another Anglican priest, gives this information regarding continental Reformed customs:

> In the churches of Lithuania and Polonia, where they have their hats on at sermon, they always put them off at the name of Jesus; and the women if they be sitting, bow down their heads; if they stand, they make a curtsy. The Reformed Church of Bremen do the like. And the same reverence was used at the naming of that holy name by a great many, though not by all, nor always, before the wars in the Palatinate, and no doubt they do so still.[4]

Meanwhile, in Switzerland, Burnet observed many Reformed faithful bowing at Jesus' name in Chür and Bern, where he also saw women facing east to pray during public prayer as well as in private devotions before and after services.[5]

Durel records that the continental Reformed knelt for prayer in the seventeenth century. Standing was also a proper token of honor to God. The Reformed of Hungary and Transylvania stood throughout the service, as did the Dutch, though 'herenbanken' were provided for Elders and the privileged.[6] The nineteenth century French Reformed stood for public prayer and sat to sing praise.[7] Scottish Presbyterians and British and American Puritans likewise stood to pray, although sitting began to infiltrate Scottish services by 1666, and, prevailed by the mid-nineteenth century in both Great Britain and the United States.[8]

---

[1] Posture for communion is excluded from this presentation.

[2] *Calvin: Institutes of the Christian Religion*, ed J. T. McNeill, Library of Christian Classics (SCM, London, 1961) 3.20.33, vol 2, p.897. Watts, GP, p.153. Cotton Mather, *The Way to Excel* (Boston, NE, 1697) stressing I Cor. 11.10.

[2] *Bishop Burnet's Travels Through France, Italy, Germany and Switzerland* . . . [1st ed 1686] (London, 1750) p.259.

[4] John Durel, *A View of the Government and Publick Worship of God in The Reformed Churches beyond the Seas* (London, 1662) p.34.

[5] *Bishop Burnet's Travels*, p.84.

[6] Durel, *op. cit.*, p.33. K. H. D. Haley, *The Dutch in the Seventeenth Century* (Thames and Hudson, London, 1972) p.86. An anon engraving illustrating A. Valerius, *Nederlantsche gedenckclanck* (1626) suggests that the Dutch knelt for prayer: reproduced in Simon Schama, *The Embarrassment of Riches: An Interpretation of Dutch Culture in the Golden Age* (Alfred Knopf, NY, 1987) p.99.

[7] Ashton Oxenden, *The History of my Life: An Autobiography* (London, 1891) p.257.

[8] *The Whole Works . . . Robert Leighton* . . . (London, 1869) vol 2, pp.440-1. Horton Davies, *The Worship of the English Puritans* (Dacre, Westminster, 1948) p.51. Julius Melton, *Presbyterian Worship in America: Changing Patterns Since 1787* (John Knox, Richmond, VA, 1967) p.38.

Calvin viewed stretching forth the hands during prayer as a declaration of taking refuge in God. French and Dutch illustrations suggest that people publicly prayed with palms pressed together.[1]

Finally, Durel mentions that the Reformed of Poland and Lithuania beat their breast at the end of prayers and stood for the creed, at which time the nobles present drew their swords 'to signify that they were ready to use them for the defence of the Christian faith.'[2]

3. FASTING AND FEASTING

Fasting, the most common medieval ascetic discipline[3], was one of the devotional practices shared by Protestant and Catholic alike across Europe.[4] Reformers saw warrants for it in the example of Jesus, the apostles and the primitive church. Calvin approved of fasting, sackcloth and ashes as useful to counteract sluggishness in devotion, though judging fasting, as all other external rites, useless, unless joined with prayer.[5] The Reformed did not limit fasting to abstinence from food and drink but extended it to include vigilance against any kind of excess in order to be subject to the Holy Spirit and not enslaved by the desires of the flesh.[6]

Fast days were observed by churches and communities, families and individuals, and at least in the private and public/civic context, survived late into the nineteenth century.[7] Fasting was used for penitence, intercession, to deepen prayer for guidance, and to prepare for the Lord's Supper. Fast days were a ritual for coping with calamity and change.[8]

---

[1] *Calvin: Iob*, p.226. Pierre Du Moulin [the Younger] *A Week of Soliloquies and Prayers* (London, 1677) frontispiece. Schama, *op. cit.*, p.99.

[2] Durel, *op. cit.*, p.37. Brandishing of swords apparently had ceased by 1662.

[3] John T. McNeill and Helena M. Gamer, *Medieval Handbooks of Penance* (Columbia University Press, NY, 1938) p.31.

[4] Flynn, *art cit*, p.266. Gildrie, *op. cit.*, p.113.

[5] J. Calvin, *Commentaries on the Book of the Prophet Daniel* (Edinburgh, 1853) vol 2, pp.137-8. See also: *Calvin Institutes*, vol 1: 3.3.17, p.611 and 3.4.11, p.635, vol 2: 4.12.17, p.1243. Sackcloth in public discipline survived in Scotland well into the eighteenth century: Sprott, *BCO*, p.1 [i.e. Roman '50].

[6] *Calvin: Deuteronomie*, p.390. *The Decades of Henry Bullinger* (Parker Society, Cambridge, 1849) vol 1, pp.428-434. Ostervald, *op. cit.*, pp.271-301. *The Westminster Directory. . .*, intro I. Breward, Grove Liturgical Study, no 21 (Grove Books, Bramcote, 1980) pp.29-30.

[7] Richard P. Gildrie, 'The Ceremonial Puritan: Days of Humiliation and Thanksgiving' in *The New England Historical and Genealogical Register* 136 (1982) pp.3-16. Horton Davies, *The Worship of the American Puritans, 1629-1730* (Peter Lang, NY, 1990) pp.58-67. Hambrick-Stowe, *op. cit.*, pp.100-103. Contrary to Rice, *op. cit.*, p.65, who states that secret fasts have been neglected since Jonathan Edwards' lifetime (1703-1758): evidence of use by the devout extends well into the nineteenth century: American Congregational minister Samuel Hopkins (1721-1803) fasted each Saturday for more than sixty years: *The Works of Samuel Hopkins* (Boston, 1852) vol 1, p.26. American Presbyterian Ashbel Green (1762-1848) fasted one day each month throughout his life and sometimes shared a fast day with his wife: *Life of Ashbel Green*, pp.565, 340. Mary Dix Gray (1810-1881) observed fast days: Clifford M. Drury, intro and ed, *First White Women Over the Rockies*, Northwest Historical Series (Arthur Clark, Glendale, CA, 1963) vol 1, p.253. However Rice is correct that the practice gradually fell into disuse (p.64).

[8] R. Baxter, *Reliquiae Baxterianae*, ed M. Sylvester (London, 1696) p.81. Burnet, *op. cit.*, pp.51-2, 132, 182, 258, 279, 302. Schmidt, *op. cit.*, pp.32-3, 76-9 and *passim*.

Reformed churches in Poland, Bohemia and Lithuania observed quarterly ember weeks with public fasting, and retained more frequent fasts, particularly during Holy Week, for the worthy reception of the Lord's Supper.[1] *The Westminster Directory* (1645) and subsequent Presbyterian directories for worship derived from it, direct public fast days to be spent in singing psalms, prayer, hearing the word read and preached, in addition to abstinence from food. Family and individual preparation were to precede the public service.[2]

The *Discipline* of the French Reformed Church provided for fasting, and 'when crises threatened to turn truly apocalyptic,' the Dutch observed 'bededagen,' both in the Netherlands and the New World.[3]

Individual 'secret' days of fasting and prayer, generally neglected in scholarly accounts, are abundantly attested in primary sources.[4]

Thanksgiving days, a ritual response to blessing and joy, were a medieval devotional custom that Reformed Christians inherited and reshaped.[5] Scripture and the life of the primitive church furnished warrants.[6] Thanksgiving days were observed in a church/community context, and by neighbourhoods, families and individuals.

If food was scarce on fast days, the Reformed enjoyed God's plenty on thanksgiving days—sometimes 'soberly,' sometimes, as in the Netherlands, with groaning tables that overwhelmed visitors.[7] Praising God with prayer and psalms, recording God's benefits in a spiritual diary, and giving gifts to the poor were also practiced.[8] Examples of thanksgiving occasions were a mother and child safely delivered through childbirth, a ship returning to port, a war's end.[9] Modern scholarship tends to overlook the role of

---

[1] Durel, *op. cit.*, pp.27-8.

[2] *Westminster Directory*, pp.29-30. Stanley R. Hall, *The American Presbyterian Directory for Worship: History of a Liturgical Strategy* (unpublished PhD dissertation, University of Notre Dame, 1990) discusses the WD and related directories.

[3] John Quick, *Synodicon in Gallia Reformata* (London, 1692) vol 1, p.xliii. Schama, *op. cit.*, p.150. Esther Singleton, *Dutch New York* (NY, 1909) pp.203-4.

[4] Hambrick-Stowe, *op. cit.*, pp.176, 281-3, is an exception. Some primary literature: [Lewis Bayly] *The Practice of Piety* (London, 1640 ed) pp.419-42. Benjamin Bennet, *The Second Part of the Christian Oratory* (London, 1728) pp.1-41. James Meikle, *Solitude Sweetened*, new ed (Edinburgh, 1843) pp.xiii-xiv, xxxi. 'Memoir of Rezeau Brown,' in *Biblical Repertory* 6 (1834) pp.444-5, and note 7 on p.16 opposite.

[5] Gildrie, *Profane*, p.113. English Puritan Thomas Becon (1512-1567) suggests that the Reformed manner of thanksgiving replaced pilgrimages, the offering of candles, and expensive gifts to the church: *The Early Works of Thomas Becon*, ed J. Ayre (Parker Society, Cambridge, 1843) 'The Pathway unto Prayer,' p.185.

[6] Oliver Heywood cites Ps. 37.4 and I Thess. 5.16 in *Advice to an Only Child*, pp.44-47. Bennet, *Second Part*, pp.42-69; warrants: Acts 2.42, 46 and many pss. Isaac Watts, *Nine Sermons* (Oxford, 1812) Sermons 8 and 9, 'The Nature and Duty of Thanksgiving,' cites I Thess. 5.18; Ps. 103.1-2, pp.161, 163.

[7] Baxter, *Reliquiae*: 'every religious woman that was safely delivered . . . if they were able, did keep a day of thanksgiving with some of their neighbours, with them, praising God, and singing psalms, and soberly feasting together.' p.83. Schama, *op. cit.*, 152.

[8] Calvin urged thanksgiving prayer morning and evening, and keeping a 'register' of God's benefits: *Calvin: Deuteronomie*, pp.455, 520, 1125. Bayly, *op. cit.*, p.444ff, 'Holy Feasting'. *Westminster Directory*, pp.31-2.

[9] E. P. Alexander, ed with intro, *The Journal of John Fontaine: An Irish Huguenot Son in Spain and Virginia, 1710-1719* (Colonial Williamsburg Foundation, Williamsburg, VA, 1972) pp.3-4. *Life of Ashbel Green*, pp.279-80.

thanksgiving in Reformed spirituality; however, again, primary sources are replete with examples.[1]

The Reformed tradition cannot be said to have a disembodied approach to worship. Though most bodily expression of prayer gradually disappeared after the eighteenth century, this was the result of cultural forces, not the fault of the Reformers.[2] They could not but glorify God in their bodies.

---

[1] For the prosecution: note *The Diary of Rev. Ralph Josselin 1616-1683*, Camden Third Series, vol 15 (Royal Historical Society, London, 1908): Ed E. Hockliffe defends printing less than half the diary of the nonconformist minister who conformed in 1662: 'There are many entries of no interest whatever—endless thanks to God for his goodness "to mee and mine," prayers, notes about the weather . . .' p.v. For the defence: Hambrick-Stowe, *op. cit.*, pp.102, 140-1. A. Peel, ed, *The Notebook of John Penry*, Camden Third Series, vol 67 (Royal Historical Society, London, 1944) p.35. Turner, *Oliver Heywood*, vol 1, p.322.

[2] Contrary to *The Oxford Encyclopedia of the Reformation*, 1996, sv 'Devotional Practices,' by Virginia Reinburg, vol 1, p.479, Reformed theologians did not 'devalue the religious meaning of the human body' nor religious practice, though they did oppose works-righteousness. See evidence cited in Karay Tripp, *op. cit.*; David Tripp, 'The Image of the Body in the Formative Phases of the Protestant Reformation' in S. Coakley, ed, *Religion and the Body: Comparative Perspectives on Devotional Practices* (Cambridge University Press, forthcoming).

4. The Psalms, the Prayer of 'Christ and All His Members'

For Zwingli and Calvin and generations of the Reformed, the psalms spoke of Christ and the church.[1] They were the people's special participation in public worship and were integral to family and individual prayer.[2] The polemic against form divorced from spiritual worship also underlies the conception of psalmody: God must be praised with heart, voice and understanding; singing without inward grace was empty ceremonial worship. Reformed folk found psalm-singing a source of refreshment and fortitude.[3] Psalms composed the mind, expressed delight in and gratitude to God, and with Col. 3.16 in mind, were useful for instruction and admonition.[4] Reformed devotion to and relish in the psalms should not be underestimated.[5]

How were psalms used? There is evidence for selective, in-course and set use. Selective use, encouraged by a patristic treatise, as well as major Reformed authorities, mined the psalter as a prayerbook. 'A Treatise made by Athanasius upon the Psalms in Anno 397'

---

[1] G. R. Potter, 'Zwingli and the Book of Psalms,' *Sixteenth Century Journal* X, 2 (1979) p.47. The Geneva Bible introduced Ps 69 'as a figure of Christ and all his members', words applicable to the other pss. For further study: Emily R. Brink, 'Metrical Psalmody: A Tale of Two Traditions' in *Reformed Liturgy & Music* 23 (Winter 1989) pp.3-8. *The Genevan Psalter 1562-1865*, ET, W. A. McComish (Bibliothèque publique et universitaire, Genève, 1986). *The New Grove Dictionary of Music & Musicians*, 1995 printing, sv 'Psalmody' by N. Temperley and R. Crawford, and 'Psalms, Metrical', by N. Temperley, H. Slenk, M. Munck and J. M. Barkley, pp.337-382. J. Julian, *A Dictionary of Hymnology* (London, 1892). Robin A. Leaver, *'Goostly psalmes and spiritual songes': English and Dutch Metrical Psalms from Coverdale to Utenhove 1535-1566* (Clarendon, Oxford, 1991). Hughes Oliphant Old, *Worship That is Reformed According to Scripture*, Guides to the Reformed Tradition, eds J. H. Leith and J. W. Kuykendall (John Knox, Atlanta, 1984) pp.39-55. Percy A. Scholes, *The Puritans and Music in England and New England* (Russell, NY, 1962). Alexander Sándor Unghváry, *The Hungarian Protestant Reformation in the Sixteenth Century Under the Ottoman Impact* (E. Mellen, Lewiston, NY, 1989) p.285, stating that the Calvinist Reformer Péter S. J. Melius (1536-72) retained congregational singing. A. T. Van Deursen, *Plain Lives in a Golden Age: Popular culture, religion and society in seventeenth-century Holland* (Cambridge University Press, Cambridge, 1991) pp.269-70, both Van Deursen and J. Moore, *A View of Society and Manners in France, Switzerland, Germany and Italy . . .* (Phil, 1783) vol 2, p.137, attest to outdoor psalmody.

[2] *The Whole Booke of Psames* [Bay Psalter] (Cambridge, NE, 1640) sigs *2ᵛ-*3ʳ. John Cotton stressed that psalms were for all people and not reserved for 'select Choristers': *Singing of Psalmes* (London, 1650) pp.39-40.

[3] Drelincourt, *op. cit.*, p.180. Cotton, *op. cit.*, pp.4-6.

[4] Cotton, *op. cit.*, p.36. Leland, *op. cit.*, p.xi.

[5] John Moore, M.D. (1729-1802) observing the Reformed (many of Huguenot descent) of Frankfurt, Germany, commented: 'The people here have a violent taste for psalm-singing': *op. cit.*, vol 2, p.137. Congregational minister Eleazar Wheelock (1711-1793) writes that Oneida Indians sang psalms in three-part harmony and many of them testified it was worthwhile to be Christian, 'if only for the pleasure of singing praise to God', D. M'Clure and E. Parrish, *Memoirs of Eleazar Wheelock, D.D.* (Newburyport, 1811; reprint ed, Arno Press, NY, 1972) p.274. African slaves in Virginia took an ecstatic delight in psalmody, and, notes Samuel Davies [Presbyterian], sometimes sang ' a torrent of sacred harmony' in his kitchen far into the night, carrying Davies too, 'away to heaven': William H. Foote, *Sketches of Virginia, Historical and Biographical*, first series, [new ed] (1st ed 1850; reprint ed, John Knox, Richmond, VA, 1966) pp.286, 289.

circulated among Puritans in at least thirty-two editions of the Sternhold-Hopkins psalter published between 1566 and 1687 (only two of these editions listed in the British Library General Catalogue were published after 1662, the year that Puritan ministers were ejected from the Church of England).[1] St Athanasius' suggestions for psalm use include: 'If thine adversary lie long in wait against thee, despair not as though God had forgotten thee, but call upon the Lord, and sing the 15, 16, 22 Psalms. If thou wilt sing to the Lord, call together God's servants on the festival day and sing the 81, 65, 134 Psalms. If thou wilt sing special of our Saviour Christ, thou hast of him in every psalm, but chiefly in the 25, 45, 110 Psalm.'[2]

In the widely-used Reformed devotional classic, *The Practice of Piety*, Lewis Bayly (1565-1631) advised that psalms could be used in order or chosen for selective use. He advised psalms 3, 5, 16, 22 and 144 in the morning, 4, 126 and 141 for evening; 19, 92 and 95 on the Sabbath. Isaac Watts suggested in-course use both in church and family while also expecting selective use and assigning each psalm a heading. Watts suggested psalms 3 and 141 for morning, evening: 4, 139 and 141; Lord's Day morning: 5, 19, 63; Lord's Day: 92, 118; daily and nightly devotion: 134; before prayer: 95, at midnight: 63. He designated a number of psalms for occasional use, such as 6 for 'complaint in sickness,' and 26 for self-examination.[3]

In general the Puritans and later nonconformists used psalms with careful attention to content and relevance, including time of day. Such a use of the psalter closely aligned their selection with the psalms that the church, at various times, has sung for the hours of prayer.[4]

---

[1] White, *Tudor Devotion*, pp.44-5, notes that the 1567 ed of the SternholdHopkins psalter [SH] contains 'The Use of the Rest of the Psalmes not comprehended in the former Table of Athanasius.' The Greek text of the 'Letter to Marcellinus' (of which the ET in SH is a condensed translation) is in J. P. Migne, ed,*Patrologia Graeca*, xxvii (Paris 1887) Cols 11-45. See also: Old, *Worship*, pp.48-9; Scholes, *op. cit.*, pp.270-271.

[2] *The Whole Booke of Psalmes* [SH] (London, 1627) sigs A6ᵛ-B4ʳ. This book concludes with prayers commonly appended to Calvin's catechism, here, apparently derived from the Church of Scotland *Book of Common Order*.

[3] *Practice of Piety*, 35th ed (Mercy Browinge, London, 1680) pp.207-9. Watts, *Psalms* (1815) unpaginated preface.

[4] For further detail on psalm and canticle use in public and household worship, see: Diane Karay Tripp, 'Daily Prayer in the Reformed Tradition: An Initial Survey' in *Studia Liturgia* 21 (1991) pp.98-104.

5. Prayer: Offering Up our Desires

Traditional Reformed prayer is consciously addressed to God the Father through Jesus Christ, Mediator and Advocate, in the Holy Spirit. Concluding trinitarian doxologies or appeals to Christ's mediation are standard.[1] The Holy Spirit made prayer possible by helping people in their weakness, teaching how and what to pray and arousing thirst for God.[2]

The Lord's Prayer provided the model for all prayer. Depending on one's theology, it was acceptable as a set prayer or functioned as a guide. Some deemed both acceptable.[3]

Early Puritans 'esteemed that manner of prayer best, where by the gift of God, expressions were varied according to present wants and occasions, yet . . . did not account set forms unlawful.' Patrick Collinson, noting the popularity of prayerbooks for family and individual use (in contrast to public worship practice in England), concluded that 'truly extempore invocation was the exception rather than the rule.'[4] Set forms were recommended for individual use and had a distinct advantage for family prayer: familiarity with a clear text could lead to greater devotion.[5]

Prayer 'without book' was a Reformed ideal and attained by many, yet there was no period without prayerbooks. These were generally considered 'helps' that would be outgrown. However by the eighteenth century prayerbook prefaces began to admit that, were not such volumes available, 'many families would live prayerless.'[6]

The Reformed, including Puritans, recognized that extempore prayer was fraught with dangers such as 'loathsome expressions,' and was as likely to offend the reverent as to be a stumbling block to the unconverted.[7] One curious outcome of long-term extempore prayer by individuals was the emergence of set family prayers.[8]

---

[1] Orton, *op. cit.*, p.44. John Norden, *A Pensive Mans Practise*, The English Experience, No 401 (London 1584; facs reprint ed: Amsterdam: Theatrum Orbis Terrarum Ltd and NY: De Capo Press, 1971) sig A.i.^{r}

[2] Calvin, *Romans*, p.224. *Calvin: Institutes*, 3.20.5, vol 2, p.855. See Wakefield, *op. cit.*, pp.80-2; Hambrick-Stowe, *op. cit.*, p.179.

[3] Henry, *Philip Henry*, p.165. Katherine Chidley, *The Ivstification of the Independant Chvrches of Christ* (London, 1641) p.31. Frelinghuysen disapproved of its rote use, as if the words had peculiar efficacy: James Tanis, *Dutch Calvinistic Pietism in the Middle Colonies: A Study in the Life and Theology of Theodore Jacobus Frelinghuysen* (M. Nijhoff, The Hague, 1967) pp.150-1.

[4] J. Geree, *The Character of an old English Pvritane* (London, 1646) sigs A2^r-p.2; Collinson, *op. cit.*, p.360; Flynn, *art cit*, p.269, neglects the many Puritans who embraced prayerbooks.

[5] eg Preston, *op. cit.*, pp.80-1. Elizabeth Joceline, *The Mothers Legacie, to her vnborn Childe* (London, 1624) p.46.

[6] Hannah Pearsall Housman (English Congregational) learned set prayers in childhood but at age thirteen, 'began to pray without form, while not entirely leaving her old forms': Richard Pearsall, *The Power and Pleasure of Divine Life*, 2nd ed (London, printed, Boston, reprinted, 1755) p.ix. Samuel Bourn, *The Christian Family Prayer Book*, 3rd ed (Birmingham, 1746) p.xxxvii.

[7] Baxter, CD, II. 23, p.462. Watts, GP, p.129.

[8] American Congregationalist Jacob Abbot's 'long custom had produced a prayer so uniform that his daughter after his death was able to write out part of it from memory.' 'Father's Prayer . . . was repeated daily at family worship:' Lyman Abbott, *Reminiscences* (Houghton Mifflin, Boston, 1923) pp.18-19.

When the Reformed prayed without forms, they considered it irreverent to be unprepared. Through scripture reading and meditation they stocked their hearts and minds with appropriate thoughts and phrasing, a technique known as 'conceived' prayer. They valued the 'gift of prayer', by which they understood a 'holy skill' that could be acquired by following certain directions, and for which the help of the Holy Spirit was indispensable.[1] The devotional language of the Bible was memorized.[2]

Both clergy and laypeople used books such as Henry's *Method for Prayer* to attain skill in prayer language.[3] Whereas many Anglicans turned to the *Book of Common Prayer*, the Reformed often carried their *book* in their heads. Late eighteenth- and nineteenth-century Reformed prayer utilized biblical language but in general lacked the imagination and freshness that characterized the prayer of earlier generations.

---

[1] Watts, GP, pp.127, 123.

[2] [J. Orton] *Memoirs of the Life, Character, and Writings of the Late Reverend Philip Doddridge* ([Shrewsbury], 1766) p.17.

[3] M. Henry, *A Method for Prayer* (London, 1710). J. Clarke, *Holy Oyle for the Lampes of the Sanctvarie* (London, 1630). *idem, Holy Incense for the Censers of the Saints. Or, a Method of Prayer* (London, 1634). N. Vincent, *The Spirit of Prayer* (London, 1674).

6. Time and Place

Prayer without ceasing in every place (I Thess. 5.17; I Tim. 2.8) was both privilege and duty.[1] Regular prayer times counteracted human weakness, laziness and worldly intrusion on spiritual affairs.[2] A superstitious view of set hours was discouraged. In part, pragmatic concerns determined the time and length of worship.[3]

The Reformed were committed to set prayer hours by the individual and family, and often, for public daily service, but these hours, typically morning and evening, were regarded as the minimum consistent with the command to pray without ceasing.[4]

Set hours were suggested by the rhythms of life, such as Calvin's list of prayer times[5]: 'when we arise in the morning, before we begin daily work, when we sit down to a meal, when by God's blessing we have eaten, when we are getting ready to retire' and by scripture: for example, Ps. 104.19-24; Ex. 29.38-42, Ps. 55.17, Dan. 6.10 and Ps. 119. 164.[6]

The Reformed have tended to deemphasize the church building as sacred space. 'We must call upon God everywhere,' preached Calvin.[7] Factors contributing to the decentralization of sacred space are caution against superstitious religious observance[8], persecution (for example, England, France, Hungary, Netherlands)[9], an increasing valuation of the natural world in creation-centred meditation[10,] and adherence to scriptural models for prayer in various locations. Over several centuries a gradual, often coerced, shift of daily prayer from church to home is detectable.

Individuals prayed in their bed-chamber or 'closet' (Mt. 6.6). The dominical term was interpreted as any place where noise and interruption were at a minimum and the suppliant might ardently pray without being overheard. The woods or open fields ('Isaac's oratory', Gen. 24.63) were also favoured prayer sites.[11] Family worship centred on the table and parlour within the home.[12]

---

[1] Calvin, *Psalms*, vol 2, pp.271-2.

[2] *Calvin: Institutes*, 3.20.50, vol 2, p.917. *Maister Beza's Hovshold Prayers*, 1607 ed, sig B10ᵛ

[3] Baxter, CD, 2.17, p.446.

[4] Baxter, CD, 2.3, p.400.

[5] *Calvin: Institutes*, 3.20.50, vol 2, pp.917-8. It seems likely that Calvin had a patristic source in mind. Thomas Becon cites an identical list of prayer times, giving Ambrose as his source: Becon, *Early Works*, 'Pathway,' p.172. See O. Faller, ed, *S. Ambrosii De Virginibus*, Florilegium Patristicum XXXI (Hanstein, Bonn, 1933) p.70, ln 23-p.71, ln 23. Both Calvin and Becon omit 'at the hour of incense'. [The author is grateful to D .H. Tripp for his work on the Latin and German sources used in this study.]

[6] Bennet, *Christian Oratory*, pp.642, 637. Baxter, CD, 2.3, p.400.

[7] *Calvin: Deuteronomie*, p.829 from a passage discouraging pilgrimages. Nevertheless, spiritual geography exerted its sway: Jesus 'felt the power of locality,' asserted German Reformed [USA] theologian Henry Harbaugh, *The Golden Censer; or, Devotions for Young Christians* (Phil, 1860) p.15. Ashbel Green, for example, chose a site by a chestnut tree for prayer: *Life of Ashbel Green*, p.127.

[8] *Calvin: Theological Treatises*, p.79. Calvin and colleagues excluded folk from local churches outside stated hours lest they enter for 'superstitious' reasons.

[9] See, eg: Horton Davies, *Worship and Theology in England* (Princeton University Press, Princeton, 1975) vol 2, pp.444-9. J. N. Ogilvie, *The Presbyterian Churches of Christendom*, new ed (London and Edinburgh, 1925) p.96.

[10] Among British and New England Puritans, Job 12.7-8, Ps. 8.3 and Rom. 1.20 furnished warrants for 'meditation upon the creatures.' Thomas Taylor, *Meditations upon the Creatures*, 3rd ed (London, 1632).

[11] Orton, *Religious Exercises*, pp.6-7.

[12] McDannell, *op. cit.*, pp.28-51, 83-4. E. Frossard, *Le Manuel des Chrétiens Protestants* (Paris, 1861) p.129.

7. Communities

1. PUBLIC ASSEMBLY

The scarcity of research into Reformed public prayer has encouraged the assumption that the subject is all but non-existent and that such services yielded to family prayers at an early date. In fact, the Reformers supported and instituted daily public services, which continued through the seventeenth century in most countries, and in some places, extended into or began in the nineteenth century (Geneva and mission settings such as Hawaii and India), and the twentieth (Aberdeen, Edinburgh, and African missions). Calvin commended common prayers to strengthen the whole church and to fortify believers' faith.[1]

John Durel describes daily services in three neglected traditions: Hesse, Hungary-Transylvania, and Lithuania-Poland. Each used a servicebook and sang the Lord's Prayer and Apostles' Creed regularly. Non-preaching services of prayer, psalms and proper readings were held each weekday noon in Hessen. Three-day feasts for the Nativity, Easter and Pentecost were observed with two services each day (most with sermons), using proper hymns. In psalmody, musicians and people together sang verses alternating with verses played by the organist. At the conclusion of worship, anthems were sung 'in consort not only with organs, but with loud instruments and violins too.'[2]

The Reformed churches of Hungary and Transylvania [Romania] worshiped each weekday morning and evening, with sermons on Wednesday and Friday only. The Old Testament was read in the morning, the New in the evening. Proper hymns were sung on festal days (the Nativity, January 1, the Resurrection, Ascension and Pentecost) and trumpets played at the church doors. The *Gloria Patri* sometimes concluded hymns. From 1677 to 1781 the Reformed of this region were persecuted; the church survived in home gatherings.[3]

Twice daily liturgical services were also held in Lithuania and Poland. The 'great litany' was said or sung each Friday, each Lenten Wednesday and on all fast days. 'Lesser litanies' were used at other times. Psalms and hymns were sung, most concluding with the *Gloria Patri*, which was also sometimes sung following the sermon, as was the *Regi seculorum*. The *Veni Sancte Spiritus* was sung frequently. The five major Reformed festivals were observed as was the Passion: collects were used for each day and hour, and for each of the *Septem verba*, our Saviour's last words. The people fasted and prayed in the church on Good Friday. Polish and Lithuanian Reformed churches observed holy days for commemoration of the blessed Virgin, the apostles, other saints and martyrs, as well as All Saints' Day. They reverenced the name of Jesus throughout worship and beat their breast at the conclusion of prayers.[4] In these vibrant traditions, the people participated vigorously through gesture, sung and spoken prayer and the hearing of the word.

---

[1] Hughes O. Old, 'Daily Prayer in the Reformed Church of Strasbourg, 1525-1530' in *Worship* 52 (1978) pp.121-38. See Karay Tripp, 'Daily Prayer,' p.192, note 13 for details on public morning and evening prayer in France until 1662, at least, daily services of the Church of Neuchâtel (through the eighteenth century); pp.196-7, note 23 for brief detail on Bern and Basel. *Calvin: Deuteronomie*, p.660.

[2] Durel, *op. cit.*, pp.26, 34-9. Hessen also observed 1 Jan (probably as New Year) and the Ascension.

[3] Durel, *op. cit.*, pp.26, 34-41. Jenö Szigeti, 'Eighteenth-Century Hungarian Protestant Pietist Literature and John Bunyan' in M. van Os and G. J. Schutte, eds, *Bunyan in England and Abroad: Papers delivered at the John Bunyan Tercentenary Symposium*, VU Studies on Protestant History, no 1 (VU University Press, Amsterdam, 1990) pp.133-4.

[4] Durel, *op. cit.*, pp.26, 34-41.

a. Zurich

Around 1685 ecclesiastical tourist Gilbert Burnet was edified to see 'great numbers' of people at morning and evening prayer all over Switzerland.[1] This study focuses on Zurich and Geneva. In Huldrych Zwingli's Zurich each church held daily services at five am and eight pm. By 1693 they were at six am and nine am; evening prayer was at five pm on Wednesday, Saturday and Sunday. Church bells summoned people to worship, and young men, running through the streets, encouraged people to attend.[2] Daily assemblies were preaching services until the late seventeenth century. Before proclaiming the word, the minister laid the book on the pulpit and knelt on the floor in silent prayer. Then, rising, he read a portion of scripture and preached 'by heart' up to forty-five minutes.[3]

Zwingli's basis for both Sunday and weekday was John Surgant's 1502 version of the medieval Prone. The conclusion to many weekday services as of 1693, 'Pray constantly . . .' is a slight revision of the conclusion to Surgant's Prone: 'Pray God for me as I will for you in the office of the holy mass.' Zwingli's basic order for daily service endured.[4] Compare the daily preaching service of *To begin and end the Sermon* (1525) combined with *Christian Order and Usage of the Churches of Zurich 1535*: 'Grace, peace and mercy of the almighty God be at all times with us poor[5] sinners.Amen:' [added 1535]; intercession (for good hearing of the word, for the nation, city and persecuted), Lord's Prayer, [Silent prayer for illumination?], reading, sermon, general confession, short prayer for pardon; [Added 1535:] Lord's Prayer, *Ave Maria*, a prayer;' [Blessing or 1693 usage?]; with the *Zurich Liturgy* (c 1693) for the six am morning service: 'Grace, peace and mercy . . .' brief prayer (for illumination, intercession), silent prayer for illumination, reading, sermon, prayer of confession, 'Absolution', Lord's Prayer, prayer; 'Pray constantly one for another. Pray to God for me, which I will also do for you. Depart in peace. And the grace of God be with you.'

In early Zurich ministers employed bidding prayers, though by 1693 set forms were in use, with the people repeating prayers after the minister.[6] Variations in structure and language were built into the liturgy.

In 1593 music was readmitted into Zurich worship, but in the late seventeenth century it was confined to the beginning and end of services on Sundays, Tuesdays and fasts, when a hymn or several psalm verses were sung. No instruments were used. Psalms were

---

[1] *Bishop Burnet's Travels*, p.84.

[2] H. G. Hageman, *Pulpit and Table: Some Chapters in the History of Worship in the Reformed Churches* (SCM, London, 1962) p.22. Ministers and laity were not always eager to attend weekday services: Bruce Gordon, *Clerical Discipline and the Rural Reformation. The Synod in Zürich, 1532-1580* (Peter Lang, Bern, etc, 1992) pp.104, 274, 144. John C. Werndly, tr, *Liturgia Tigurina* (London, 1693) pp.ii-xiv, 6-7.

[3] *Ibid*, pp.5-6. Gordon, *op. cit.*, p.133 notes than in the sixteenth century ministers were required to read sermons aloud from books in order to restrict doctrinal error.

[4] See J. Neil Alexander, 'Luther's Reform of the Daily Office' in *Worship* 57 (1983) pp.356-7. Hageman, *op. cit.*, p.17. Zwingli (1484-1531) 'Die predig anzufahen und zuo enden' (1525) and 'Christenlich ordnung und bruech der kilchen Zurich' (1535) in Leonhardt Fendt, *Einführung in die Liturgiewissenschaft* (Töpelmann, Berlin, 1958) pp.227-8. Werndly, *op. cit.*, pp.1-6, 31ff. Items reserved to Sunday here omitted.

[5] Werndly, *ibid*, translates as 'miserable' and below, 'absolution'.

[6] *Ibid*, sig A6ʳ.

sung in course, in four-part harmony.[1] Around 1523 Zurich observed the Nativity, Circumcision (or New Year?), the Resurrection and Easter Monday, the Ascension, Pentecost and Whit-Monday, as well as three feasts of the Blessed Virgin Mary (Purification, Annunciation and Assumption) and a number of saints' days. In 1526 the Marian feasts and those of the saints were eliminated, though the Virgin and saints were to be commemorated in weekday sermons. The Zurich Liturgy (c 1693) provides forms to be added to the ordinary services for the day after the Nativity, New Year's Day, Easter Monday, Ascension and Pentecost. Zurich also observed Holy Week, termed, 'Holy Easter-week' with prayers and sermons each day in all churches.[2]

b. Geneva

Calvin felt that the people should assemble each morning and evening to pray and hear God's word. Though early efforts met with 'contempt and apathy', Geneva had weekday services from Calvin's time well into the nineteenth century on Monday, Tuesday and Friday, at least, probably at the hours of four am and six pm [1564]. A fine was imposed on those absent with no good excuse.[3]

The basis for public daily prayers seems to have been Calvin's *Form of Church Prayers* (1542) [FCP], a discretionary liturgy. Hageman suggests that pastors kept close to form due to various pressures. The FCP order: 'Our help is in the name of the Lord, who made heaven and earth. Amen'; bidding to confession, prayer of confession, psalm, prayer for illumination, reading, sermon, exhortation to prayer, prayer of intercession, Lord's Prayer (paraphrase), Apostles' Creed (by minister), psalm and Aaronic blessing.[4] A slight variant of the FCP, supposedly regularly used by Calvin is found at the conclusion of an English translation of Calvin's sermons on Job.[5]

---

[1] Hageman, *op. cit.*, p.21, citing F. Schmidt-Clausing, *Zwingli als Liturgiker* (Vandenhoeck und Ruprecht, Göttingen, 1955) pp.128ff. Werndly, *op. cit.*, pp.7, 17-8.

[2] Herman A. Daniel, *Codex Liturgicus, T III . . . Ecclesiae Reformatae* (Leipzig, 1851) p.23 lists the following sanctoral observances: 'Feasts of all apostles,' St Stephen, All Saints, St John the Baptist, Mary Magdalen, and Felix and Regula, patron saints of Zurich. Werndly, *op. cit.*, pp.153, 162-3.

[3] *Calvin: Deuteronomie*, pp.203-4, 207, 660. Philip E. Hughes, ed and tr, *The Register of the Company of Pastors of Geneva in the Time of Calvin* (Wm B. Eerdmans, Grand Rapids, Mich, 1966) pp.91, 362, 54. Baird, *op. cit.*, pp.32-3. 'Draft Ecclesiastical Ordinances' by Calvin et al, 1541: 'on working days there will be a sermon at St Peter three times a week on Monday, Tuesday and Friday. . .' in *Calvin: Theological Treatises*, p.62. Reid emends Tuesday (note 24) to Wednesday. However the 1712 Geneva 'Form of Prayer' (see note 132, below) clearly stipulates Tuesday. Paul Henry, *The Life and Times of John Calvin*, tr H. Stubbing, (London, 1849), vol 1, pp.418-9, states that very early there was no evening service because of desire to suppress the connection of the vesper bell with the Angelus. Durel, *op. cit.*, 1662, attests to pm worship.

[4] Hageman, *op. cit.*, p.38. The FCP outline is drawn from Bard Thompson, *Liturgies of the Western Church* (World Pub Co, Cleveland/NY, 1961) pp.197ff.

[5] Order from *Sermons on Job*: [Our help. . .?], bidding prayer (penitential and for illumination), Lord's Prayer, [reading], [sermon], bidding, variable collect, prayer of intercession, LP, Apostles' Creed, Blessing: 'The grace of God the Father and the peace of our Lord Jesus Christ through the fellowship of the Holy Ghost dwell with us for ever. Amen:' *Calvin: Iob*, pp.821-2. Baird, *op. cit.*, p.70, translates 'us' in the blessing as 'you'. Golding does not list psalms but assumes they were used in a location similar to the FCP.

Psalms were used according to 'tables; ' the psalter was sung through twice a year. The Genevan psalter, prepared at Calvin's request, completed in 1562, and used in Geneva and France, provided a collect after each psalm. These prayers, written by Augustin Marlorat, a French pastor, appeared in psalter editions until at least 1674. Presumably they were used in public daily prayer.[1]

Around 1685 Burnet attended Genevan daily prayer and deemed the sermons 'generally too long.' Possibly by 1712 and certainly by 1814 exposition was omitted.[2]

c Electoral Palatinate (Germany)

The liturgy of the Electoral Palatinate, drawn up in 1563 by Ursinus and Olevianus, and widely used by the Reformed in Germany, saw three editions by 1684 with few changes.[3] There were three kinds of weekday services.

Morning and evening prayer-sermons were to be held on all working days in towns. Lasting about half an hour, they focused on a chapter of scripture and a simple summary of doctrine. No psalms or hymns were sung. Both the bidding prayer before the sermon and the prayers following the doctrine summary were essentially those of Calvin.[4] These liturgical services may be outlined thus: 'Grace, peace and mercy from God the Father, and his beloved Son Jesus Christ our Lord together with the communion of the Holy Spirit be with us all. Amen,' or the Grace (2 Cor. 13.13); exhortation to prayer, bidding prayer of confession and for illumination, Lord's Prayer, chapter of scripture, brief summary, invitation to prayer ('Beloved in the Lord Jesus Christ. . .'), Morning Prayer or Evening Prayer, Lord's Prayer, Decalogue (am only); Apostles' Creed (pm only) Aaronic blessing.

Weekday 'sermons' were held on Wednesday and Friday in towns, and Wednesday or another day in villages. They differed from the *Gebetts-predigt* chiefly in providing a full sermon and in the singing of German psalms or hymns before and after the sermon, chosen according to the season and sermon topic.[5]

Finally, on the first Wednesday of each month, the people assembled for penitential 'sermons on days of prayer.' The sermon was shortened to allow time for extended intercessory prayer. Penitential psalms were sung.

---

[1] *Les Pseavmes de David* (Geneva, 1577) sig [viiʳ]ff: 'Table Povr Trovver Les Pseavmes . . .'; P. Pidoux, *Le Psautier Huguenot* (Bäerenreiter, Bâle, 1962), vol 2: pp.2, 134-5. *Les CL Pseaumes de Dauid. Mis en rime Francoise par Clement Marot et Theodore de Beze . . . une Oraison a la fin d'un chacun Pseaume par M. Augustin Marlorat* (Lyon, 1564). *Les Pseaumes . . .* (Charenton, 1674).

[2] *Bishop Burnet's Travels*, p.49. In 1712 an ET of the 'Prayers That are to be read in the Church of Geneva on Monday Evening, Tuesday Morning, and Friday Evening' was published in J. F. Osterwald, *The Liturgy used in the Churches of the Principality of Neufchatel* (London, 1712) pp.102-16. The set orders revise the FCP and omit exposition. Provisions are made for proper prayers for three-day celebrations of Christmas, Easter, Ascension, Pentecost and New Year's Day. This must have been part of the revision in progress by the Genevan Church, completed in 1723 and published in the Psalter of 1725, providing prayers for Mon pm, Tues am, Wed am and pm, Fri am and Sat am and pm; and introducing prayers for the festal days just mentioned. See: *Genevan Psalter*, ch 13 (unpaginated). Richard B. Bernard, *A Tour Through Some Parts of France, Switzerland, Savoy, Germany and Belgium . . . 1814* (Phil, 1815) p.135.

[3] *Chur-Pfaelzische Kirchen-Ordnung* (Heidelberg, 1684) sig iiʳ⁻ᵛ. Hageman, *op. cit.*, pp.32-3. E. Sehling *et al*, eds, *Die evangelischen Kirchenordnungen, Bd XIV: Kurpfalz* (Mohr, Tübingen, 1969) pp.333-408.

[4] *Chur-Pfaelzische KO*, pp.10-11, 204, 211-20.

[5] *Ibid*, pp.2-3, 7, 166ff, 280.

From 1563 the following feasts were observed: Christmas and the day following, New Year's Day, Easter and Easter Monday, Ascension, Pentecost and Whit-Monday. Good Friday entered the calendar by 1684.[1]

d. Scotland

Weekday services in all town and many village churches were general in Scotland from 1560 until 1645. *The First Book of Discipline* [FDB] drawn up in 1560 by Knox and others provided for two kinds of daily service: preaching and 'Common Prayers.'

Sermon-plus-prayers were usually observed on Wednesday and Friday; 'notable towns' were required to have a weekday service. Scripture was to be read in English, in course. The 1564 Book of Common Order [BCO] allowed discretionary use of the liturgy.[2]

The FDB also directed that there be 'Common Prayers, ' with some exercise of reading of scripture, leaving the frequency of assembly to individual kirks. In 1595 the Glasgow kirk session, for example, stipulated daily prayers in the High Kirk at seven am and in the New Church at five p.m.[3] These services,[4] very general in Scotland, were led by 'readers'— at first, mainly ex-priests who continued to serve their former parishes; later, schoolmasters, catechists and candidates for the ministry.

The 'Reader's Service', or 'Common Prayers', generally consisted of psalms (including metrical versions of other scripture), prayers and scripture. The 1552 *Book of Common Prayer* appears to have been used until around 1562. By 1559 the 'Book of Geneva, was used by some congregations, and in 1564, the BCO, a modified and enlarged version of the Genevan Order, was published and remained the rule of worship until superseded by the Westminster Directory in 1645. Prayers from the BCO 'Order of Public Service' and also from the domestic prayer section at the end of the book were used in Common Prayers.[5] It is possible that psalms were sung in course. There are also instances of set psalmody. Melville, for example, mentions that while he was a student at St Andrews, the principal commonly used psalms 44 and 79 in daily prayers.[6]

Daily public prayers were suppressed by the mid-seventeenth century. The blame has been variously pinned on the Privy Council, acting on a report from the bishops that limited daily worship to preaching days, the Westminster Directory, or ministers influenced by English Independents.[7] In the late seventeenth century, in some areas of Scotland, ministers

---

[1] *Ibid*, pp.7-8. Sehling, *op. cit.*, p.397.

[2] G. W. Sprott, ed, *Scottish Liturgies of the Reign of James VI* (Edinburgh, 1871) p.92. W. McMillan, *The Worship of the Scottish Reformed Church, 1550-1638* (James Clarke, London, [1931]) pp.146-7. [W. Dunlop], *A Collection of the Confessions of Faith* (Edinburgh, 1722) vol 2, pp.582-5. Sprott, *BCO*, pp.91-2.

[3] Dunlop, *op. cit.*, vol 2: pp.582-3. Sprott, BCO, p.xxliii, citing Wodrow, *Life of Weems*, p.22.

[4] See Sprott, *ibid*, pp.xxi-xxxv. McMillan, *op. cit.*, pp.136-50.

[5] Dunlop, *op. cit.*, vol 2, p.583. McMillan, *op. cit.*, pp.22, 29-30, 137, 140. *Diary of Mr. James Melville (1556-1601)*, Bannatyne Club 34 (1829) pp.125-7: 'The Order and Manner of Exercise of the Word . . .' (1584) used by Presbyterian ministers who fled to England: weekday sermons on Wed and Fri, 10-11 am; half-hour 'daily common prayers' at 10 am and 4 pm, during which a psalm was 'read and handled.'

[6] McMillan, *op. cit.*, p.136. *James Melville*, p.22. *cf* Sprott, *Scottish Liturgies*, pp.122, 126.

[7] McMillan, *op. cit.*, pp.142-3.

were forced by the government from the churches into 'conventicles' in houses, barns and fields.[1]

Nonetheless, daily prayer was not completely snuffed out. Welsh-American Samuel Davies commended Glasgow magistrates for attending public worship on weekdays as well as Sunday, c 1754. St. Giles' Cathedral, Edinburgh, has had almost continuous daily prayer since the time of John Knox.[2] There were renewed daily services in some areas as part of the Scots liturgical revival in the second half of the nineteenth century.[3] Daily services are being held in a number of major Church of Scotland parishes in the late twentieth century. The *Book of Common Order of the Church of Scotland* (1994) provides 'A Daily Service' primarily for use in church.[4]

e. England and North America
Sixteenth century Reformed refugees in England held weekday services. Several London 'Stranger' churches worshipped on Tuesday and Thursday apparently using John à Lasco's *Forma ac ratio* (1555) in translation as a worship directory.[5] Valérand Poullain and the Walloon congregation in Glastonbury had daily services in 1551. Later, in Frankfurt, when his Walloon congregation shared the Weissfrauenkirche with English exiles, Poullain's group observed hour-long services, with sermon, at daybreak on Tuesday and Thursday, the English holding service on other days.[6]

[1] Marilyn J. Westerkamp, *Triumph of the Laity: Scots-Irish Piety and the Great Awakening, 1625-1760* (Oxford University Press, NY and Oxford, 1988) pp.51-60.
[2] G. W. Pilcher, ed and intro, *The Reverend Samuel Davies Abroad: The Diary of a Journey to England and Scotland, 1753-55* (University of Illinois Press, Urbana, 1967) p.102. 14 May 1991 and 9 July 1996 telephone conversations with the Revd. J. Christopher Ledgard, Asst Minister, St Giles', 1991-92: since the early 1980's: noon service (scripture, brief homily [optional], and prayer).
[3] Hageman, *op. cit.*, pp.71-5. [Cameron Lees] *A Book of Common Order* (Edinburgh, 1884) was used at St Giles' Cathedral from 1884 to 1926 in daily services. In 1895-7, Trinity Congregational Church, Glasgow had daily service: L. S. Hunter, *John Hunter, D.D.: A Life* (London, 1921) p.93.
[4] J. G. G. Fleming, *Prayers for Every Day* (Allenson, London, 1938) p.7 notes that as of 1938 the East Church of St Nicholas, Aberdeen, had observed weekday worship with almost unbroken continuity since 1560. Springburn Parish Church, Glasgow, 11am daily service: 'Elders keep up a daily service,' *Life and Work: The Record of the Church of Scotland* (October 1990) p.11. St Giles' instituted a daily eucharist (M-F, 8am; Sat, 6pm, in addition to Sundays) in the fall, 1992. St George's and St Andrew's Parish Church, Edinburgh (1.30pm daily service). St Mary's Church, Haddington, East Lothian (noon service with preaching, summer at least). Dunblane Cathedral (midday prayer). Govan Old Parish, Glasgow (daily, begun in the 1930's by George MacLeod, who subsequently founded the Iona Community. Glasgow Cathedral also has a daily service. These services have been observed since at least 1991. Source, see note 2 above, Ledgard. *BCO* (Saint Andrew Press, Edinburgh, 1994) pp.509-520.
[5] Bryan D Spinks, *From the Lord and 'The Best Reformed Churches . . .'* (Edizioni Liturgiche, Roma, 1984) p.105: an ET of *Forma ac Ratio*, pp.157-76. Noting rubrics gives this weekday order: exhortation to prayer, prayer before sermon, Lord's Prayer, psalm, scripture reading (*lectio continua*), sermon, notices, prayer after sermon, general prayer for the church and Lord's Prayer, psalm, commendation of the poor, Aaronic blessing, collection of alms.
[6] W. D. Maxwell, *The Liturgical Portions of the Genevan Service Book* (Faith Press, London, 1965) p.11, no 5, p.103, nn 13-14, p.103, no 13 cites an excerpt from *Liturgia sacra* 1554 ed, giving Tuesday/Thursday order: psalm sung, prayer for illumination, scripture, sermon, short extempore prayer, blessing, people dismissed for work.

Likewise, English exiles in Europe gathered for weekday assemblies. The Marian exiles in Geneva held service on Monday, Tuesday and Wednesday at nine am, beginning in 1555. Italian refugees who shared the Church of Marie la Nove with the English, held services on the other weekdays.[1] Marian exiles in Emden (north Germany) met on Wednesday and Friday, beginning in 1554.[2]

Puritans adopted two strategies to deal with the perceived defects of the *Book of Common Prayer*. Modified Puritan editions of the BCP appeared illegally between 1578 and 1640; those who used them risked severe penalties.[3] Some early Puritans attended daily office in their parish churches. In a 1579 pamphlet, Robert Openshaw described a Puritan family who worshipped at their church twice each Sabbath and once each weekday. When their minister was restrained, they began family prayers instead.[4] No doubt this was not an isolated incident.

The other strategy was use of a Calvinist Reformed liturgy. The 1556 *Genevan Service Book* [GSB] of the English exiles and its modified editions printed by Waldegrave (1584) and in Middleburg (surviving eds: 1586, 1587, 1602) envisioned daily prayer according to a discretionary use of the liturgy.[5]

Elizabethan and later Puritans and nonconformists engaged in a variety of word-centered meetings[6] which must enter any consideration of the Reformed daily office. 'Exercise'—a sermon with prayers and psalms—was followed by 'conference' and dinner. There were also market-town exercises, occasional preaching fasts, catechizings, 'lectures', and prayer meetings.[7]

When Puritans were deprived of their minister or were alienated from their parish church for any reason, they gathered in homes and other secluded settings. The 'Conventicle Act' of 1664 made gatherings of five or more people over age sixteen for religious purposes illegal.[8] Despite intense persecution, Puritans continued to worship. 'Lectures' and prayer meetings were diligently attended throughout the seventeenth century and at least into

---

[1] Maxwell, *op. cit.*, p.7, citing *Registre du conseil*, vol 1, p.46. Spinks, *op. cit.*, pp.113, 131, notes GSB use by the congregation in Plumber's Hall, London, in 1567, and in 1568 by Puritans in Goldsmith's House. The Middleburg book was used by English exiles in the Netherlands, and its use is assumed among some Puritans in England.

[2] Andrew Pettegree, *Marian Protestantism* (Scolar Press, Aldershot, 1996) pp.18, 173.

[3] Spinks, *op. cit.*, pp.25-8. W. K. Clay, ed, *Liturgical Services. Liturgies and Occasional Forms of Prayer Set Forth in the Reign of Queen Elizabeth* (Parker Society, Cambridge, 1847) pp.xv-xix noting such changes as substitution of 'For Morning' and 'For Evening' for 'Mattins' and 'Evensong' in the Table of Proper Lessons in 1578 ed published by C Barker; pp.435-55: 1561 Calendar with Puritan supplements.

[4] Puritan Thomas Tymme encouraged attendance at common prayers: *Chariot of Deuotion* (London, 1618) p.35. [Robert Openshaw] *Short questions and answeares* (London, 1614) sig A5ᵛ.

[5] Maxwell, *op. cit.*, p.92. P. Hall, ed, *Reliquiae Liturgicae* (Bath, 1847) vol 1, p.xi.

[6] Collinson, *op. cit.*, pp.208-21, 372-82.

[7] See Claire Cross, *The Puritan Earl: The Life of Henry Hastings, Third Earl of Huntingdon, 1536-1595* (Macmillan, London, 1966) p.132. In Kidderminster, Hannah Housman combined shopping and worship on market-days that were also lecture-days. In 1711 she notes, 'It hath been a Market Day for Soul & Body ...' Pearsall, *op. cit.*, pp.78, 36, 76. Thomas Cranfield (1758-1838) arranged countless prayer meetings: [R. Cranfield] *The Useful Christian: A Memoir of Thomas Cranfield* (London, [1844?]) p.53.

[8] Collinson, *op. cit.*, pp.376, 379. Davies, *Worship and Theology in England*, vol 2: pp.447-49.

the mid-nineteenth century a mid-week sermon and Monday night prayer meeting were universal among Congregational churches.[1]

New England Puritans attended lectures, worship services consisting of lengthy prayer, psalmody and the proclamation of the word.[2] Puritan missionaries to Native Americans conducted lectures in the native tongue; and there were also various settings for weekday worship among Native Americans into the nineteenth century.[3] Congregationalists and Presbyterians observed lectures and prayer meetings through the same time-frame.[4]

The early Dutch Reformed colonists of New Netherland [later, New York] relied on lay pastors known as 'comforters of the sick' [*ziekentrooster*] to lead 'common prayers' each morning and evening. These services probably consisted of prayers from the liturgy, scripture and sometimes a sermon from an approved book such as Heinrich Bullinger's popular *Huysboeck* [*Decades*, 1577], commentary on the Ten Commandments, the Apostles' Creed and the sacraments. Beginning in September 1857 under the auspices of the North Dutch Church [NYC] consistory, an ecumenical prayer meeting met daily at noon for twenty-five years.[5]

f. Mission Settings

The first known Reformed worship service in the New World was daily prayer, celebrated on Wednesday, 10 March 1557 on an island in Guanabara Bay [Rio de Janeiro]. The Calvinist minister, Pierre Richer, presided. According to the French Reformed order, there was an invocation,' psalm 5 (sung), scripture and a sermon, with prayers following. Thereafter public prayers were held every evening after work.[6] Along with family and private prayer, public daily prayer seems to have featured wherever Reformed people ventured.

---

[1] R. Tudor Jones, *Congregationalism in England 1662-1962* (Independent Press, London, 1962) pp.86, 128, 227.

[2] Hambrick-Stowe, *op. cit.*, pp.99ff.

[3] Henry Whitfield, *The Light appearing more and more towards the perfect Day* (London, 1651) p.13. M'Clure and Parrish, *op. cit.*, pp.32-3 documents morning and evening school prayers. [Presbyterian] Stephen Riggs, *Tah-koo Wah-Kan; Or, The Gospel Among the Dakotas* (Boston, 1869; reprint ed, Arno Press, NY, 1972) p.358, evening prayer meetings, 1862-3.

[4] G. W. Bethune, *Memoirs of Mrs. Joanna Bethune* (NY, 1863) pp.60, 244. Abbott, *op. cit.*, pp.129-131. See also: Theology and Ministry Worship Unit, for the Presbyterian Church (U.S.A.) and the Cumberland Presbyterian Church, *Book of Common Worship* (Westminster/John Knox, Louisville, 1993) pp.489-595: 'Daily Prayer' in *The Psalter: Psalms and Canticles for Singing* (Westminster/John Knox, Louisville, 1993).

[5] Gerald F. De Jong, *The Dutch Reformed Church in the American Colonies*, Historical Series of the Reformed Church in America, No 5 (Wm B Eerdmans, Grand Rapids, 1978) pp.11-17. S. Irenaeus Prime, *Prayer and Its Answer: Illustrated in the First Twenty-Five Years of the Fulton Street Prayer Meeting* (NY, 1882): because of its longevity, the North Dutch meeting cannot be dismissed as a temporary phenomenon: cf, the 'Prayer Meeting Revival of 1857-8' of urban businessmen facing financial crisis, W. G. McLoughlin, *Revivals, Awakenings, and Reform: An Essay on Religion and Social Change in America, 1607-1977* (University of Chicago Press, Chicago, 1978) pp.141-2. The German Reformed Church (composed largely of Palatinate refugees, and under the jurisdiction of the Reformed Church of the Netherlands until 1792) seems to have had daily services. Extent unknown. See, eg, Henry Harbaugh, *Youth in Earnest; As Illustrated in the Life of Theodore David Fisher* (Phil, 1867) p.199: Fisher (1838-1863) 'was regular in his attendance on the week-day services of the church . . .' in Lebanon, PA.

[6] Janet Whatley, tr and intro, *Jean De Léry. History of a Voyage to the Land of Brazil* (University of California Press, Berkeley, 1990) pp.34-5. Calvinists had departed from the colony within one year.

In the Hawaiian Islands, nineteenth century Congregational missionaries were delighted with the healthy attendance at daily prayer meetings (often, preaching services) on various islands over many years, as well as neighbourhood meetings in 'prayer houses'. Hiram Bingham (1789-1869) wrote that the congregation in Kailua, Hawaii, (c 1834) met at five am (well before sunrise) for an hour service.[1] In the same century, Reformed Dutch [USA] missionaries in and near Madras, India, held daily preaching services; and native Presbyterians in the New Hebrides [Vanuatu] assembled for evening village prayers under a banyan tree, singing five or six hymns interspersed with short prayers.[2]

In the twentieth century Reformed missionaries led daily services at various African mission locations: the Ibanche and Luebo Mission Stations (Congo) had 'sunrise services' with several hundred attending; the Lupwe Station (northern Nigeria) had worship at six am; and at the Ocilesco Station of the West Africa Mission there were evening 'village prayers'; attendance was required of catechumens.[3]

2. FAMILY WORSHIP

Family worship was a common practice among the Reformed into the nineteenth century, with some churches preserving it through the twentieth.[4] Missionaries introduced family prayers to people they evangelized, and, since domestic worship and table prayer were conspicuous features of missionaries' lives, native people often embraced these practices 'as the first outward tokens of Christian discipline'.[5]

Consistent patterns emerged across national boundaries and were durable: family worship has typically combined scripture reading, sometimes with exposition[6], psalms or hymns, and prayer.

---

[1] Rufus Anderson, *The Hawaiian Islands*, 2nd ed (Boston, 1854) pp.293-3. Bingham, *Residence of Twenty-One Years in the Sandwich Islands*, 3rd ed (Canandaigua, NY, 1855) pp.458, 476-7.

[2] Corwin, *op. cit.*, pp.210, 390. J. Paton, ed, *The Story of John G. Paton*, rev A. K. Langridge (Hodder and Stoughton, London, [1923?]) pp.182-3.

[3] Julia Lake Kellersberger, *A Life for the Congo: The Story of Althea Brown Edmiston* (Revell, NY, 1947) pp.14, 87. Johanna Veenstra, *Pioneering for Christ in the Sudan* (Smitter, Grand Rapids, 1926) p.166. Mary Floyd Cushman, *Missionary Doctor: The Story of Twenty Years in Africa* (Harper, NY, 1944) pp.20, 97, 109, 216.

[4] Limited space precludes listing music resources.

[5] Paton, *op. cit.*, p.167. C. Mather cites an apparently contemporary account that Dutch Reformed pastors baptized 300,000 Ceylonese, teaching them the LP, Creed, Commandments, a morning and evening prayer, and grace before and after the meal, applicable both to family and individual devotion: *The Triumph of the Reformed Religion in America: The Life of the Renowned John Eliot* (Boston, 1691) p.94. Anderson, *op. cit.*, pp.84, 136-7, 293-4. Bingham, *op. cit.*, pp.200, 523. English Congregational missionary and martyr, John Williams (1796-1839) attests to am and pm family prayer among Tahitians and Samoans: E. Prout, *Memoirs of the Life of the Rev John Williams, Missionary to Polynesia* (NY, 1843) pp.35, 50, 357. For an African example, see: Kellersberger, *op. cit.*, pp.15, 110-111. For an account [c 1920] among Presbyterian missionaries with Chinese servants, see: John Espey, *Minor Heresies, Major Departures: A China Mission Boyhood* (University of California Press, Berkeley, 1994) pp.47-9.

[6] Exposition or the reading of a sermon has proved to be one of the most enduring elements of the family office. The assertion (ie by Hughes O. Old, 'The Reformed Daily Office: A Puritan Perspective' in *Reformed Liturgy & Music* 12.4 (1978) p.10) that there was no 'preaching' in Reformed homes requires serious qualification. While the 'Directory for Family Worship' (1647) of the Church of Scotland underscores that interpreting scripture is reserved to ministers (Dunlop, *op. cit.*, vol 1, p.450), note:

[continued on p.33 opposite]

For the Reformed, family worship was of ancient foundation. Joshua 24.15 was the most frequently cited warrant. New Testament families and primitive house churches also demonstrated that worship was a domestic obligation to which biblical precepts regarding the nature and frequency of prayer applied.[1] Generally, the male head of household presided in the *ecclesiola*, representing Christ's offices of prophet, priest and king.[2]

Standard elements of family worship in Calvin's Geneva and among French Reformed included a chapter of scripture, often with the reading of a sermon (for example, those of Calvin), and prayer, concluding with the Lord's Prayer and the Apostles' Creed. Though not specified in early sources, psalmody may be assumed.[3]

Calvin commended prayer before and after meals, appealing chiefly to I Tim. 4.5, which he read as showing that meals should be accompanied by scripture and prayer. A psalm was sung with meals.[4] A deliberate reformation of the medieval meal-office seems likely.[5] Calvin was further concerned for reverent conduct: 'our God is present at the table with us.'[6]

'Legislation is better evidence for what it proposes to prohibit than for what it seeks to promote,' Paul F. Bradshaw, *The Search for the Origins of Christian Worship: Sources and Methods for the Study of Early Liturgy* (Oxford University Press, NY/Oxford, 1992) p.68. The Reformed have interpreted scripture in family gatherings into the twentieth century. After a chapter, 'thou mayest admonish them of some remarkable good notes,' writes Bayly: his marginal note: 'Origen would have the word expounded in Christian houses—Hom.9 in Levit. Augustine saith, that which the Preacher is in the Pulpit, the same the Householder is in the house.' [no source] *Practice of Piety*, 1680 ed, p.195. See: M. Borret, ed, tr, *Origène, Homélies sur le Lévitique*, II, Sources Chrétiennes, 287 (Cerf, Paris, 1981) pp.94-6, Hom ix.5: 'Optamus tamen ut vel his auditis operam detis non solum in Ecclesia audire verba Dei, sed et in domibus vestris exerceri et meditari in lege Domini die ac nocte.'

The Geneva Bible marginal gloss to Gen. 17.23: 'Masters in their houses ought to be as preachers to their families,' (*The Bible and Holy Scriptures* (R. Hall, Geneva, 1560) *ad. loc.*) Puritan layman John Bruen (1560-1625) was described by his pastor as 'instructing. . . his family out of the word of God, as a pastor and teacher in his own house': William Hinde, *A Faithful Remonstrance of the Holy Life and Happy Death of John Bruen* (London, 1641) p.74. Ecclesiastical concerns regarding 'private meetings' are not denied. Note the balance of [Oliver Heywood] *A Family Altar Erected to the Honour of the Eternal God* (London, 1693) p.128-9, who answered the query, 'Whether may an house-holder take upon him to preach, expound scripture?' with the reply that the master must teach all under his charge [Deut. 11.18-21] yet remain in subordination to ministerial instruction. Then he suggests that masters 'teach' from experience, within their limits, and stick to practical truths.

[1] Warrants: Matt. 26.18-30, Luke 9.18, Acts 10.2, 21.5, I Cor. 16.9: Gouge, *Word to Sinners* pp.220-34.

[2] Baxter, CD, 2.3., p.389. J. Alexander, *Thoughts on Family Worship* (Phil, 1847) p.193.

[3] Henry, *John Calvin*, vol 1, pp.361, 435-6, 440. C. Marot and Th. de Bèze, *Pseavmes de David* (1577), sigs Ggvi[v] ff, 'L'Exercise Dv Pere de famille, & de tous ses domestiques pour prier au matin.' *Le Psautier de Genève 1562-1865* (Bibliothèque publique et universitaire, Genève, 1986) pp.86-[90]; Paul de Félice, *Les Protestants d'Autrefois* (Paris, 1897) pp.77-90. Hageman, *op. cit.*, pp.51-2: sermons were still used in mid-eighteenth century France. Frossard, *op. cit.*, p.128, in 1861 indicates that reading from an 'edifying book' was optional for Sunday.

[4] Calvin, *Timothy*, pp.105-6; Baird, *op. cit.*, pp.80-1.

[5] See Karay Tripp, 'Daily Prayer,' pp.207-8, note 64. The LP was used before and after meals in the Palatinate (Dunlop, *op. cit.*, vol 2, pp.357-8), Zurich (Werndly, *op. cit.*, p.23), Holland, Transylvania and Hungary (Durel, *op. cit.*, p.36) probably reflecting pre-Reformation custom.

[6] *Calvin: Deuteronomie*, p.567. Warrant: Deut. 14.26b.

The twice-daily worship of Elizabethan Puritans consisted of the reading of scripture, (preceded by a brief prayer for illumination), psalm-singing, prayer, (Lord's Prayer, often, and Creed, sometimes included) and might end with the Aaronic blessing ('us') or the Grace. Catechetical instruction and admonition (Heb. 3.13) might be included, especially in the evening. Sermons such as those of Calvin and Henry Smith were often read.[1] The meal-office was seen in a eucharistic context: Puritans prayed and sang psalms at mealtime after Jesus' example[2] and that of the primitive church (Eph. 5.19-20). The grace after the meal often doubled as a prayer for illumination, at the same time including brief intercession.[3] Concern for sober conduct and godly table-talk (Eph. 4.29) were strong in this period.[4]

Although family worship in the seventeenth-century remained much the same as before,[5] the plethora of devotional books[6] offer more detailed accounts. The Bible was read through annually, in-course, a chapter of the Old Testament in the morning, at worship before breakfast, and one of the New during evening, after supper. Exposition of the chapter might follow, or family Bible study, catechism, a reading from a 'godly book' or recollection of sermons from the previous Lord's Day.[7] Psalms were sung in course, but were also used with attention to content, with certain psalms favoured for morning and evening.[8] At least in the early part of the century, meals were accompanied with prayer and psalms, with a chapter of scripture read at noon.

The eighteenth century saw a decline in the practice of family worship, although Philip Doddridge did much to revitalize it.[9] Changes in this century include the introduction of hymns, a tendency for exposition to be used on the Lord's Day evening only, if at all[10]; the chapter and psalm dropped from meal time.

---

[1] Openshaw, *op. cit.*, sigs A5ᵛ-C3ʳ. Morgan, *op. cit.*, p.155. *Works of Henry Smith.*

[2] Smith, *op. cit.*, vol 1, pp.45-6. Mk 14.26 was also cited. Richard Stocke, *The Churches Lamentation . . . a Sermon, at the Funeral of . . . Iohn Lord Harrington* (London, 1614) p.79.

[3] [Stephen Egerton], *A Brief Method of Catechizing*, 22nd ed (London, 1615) pp.50-3. Openshaw, *op. cit.*, sigs A6ʳ⁻ᵛ

[4] *Works of Henry Smith*, vol 1, p.299; vol 2, pp.12-13, 355.

[5] Henry, *Philip Henry*, pp.86-98 describes Henry family worship c 1670: short prayer; metrical psalms, in order; chapter (in-course), exposition and brief discussion; prayer (with reference to family circumstances; doxology), benediction; children's prayer for God's blessing on parents. Lord's Day worship closed with Ps 134. Pss with meals reserved to Lord's Day. No mention of Creed used in England by this date.

[6] eg [John Brinsley, the Elder] *The Fovrth Part of the Trve Watch* (London, 1624) sigs Vff lists 197 'Protestant helpes for Deuotion.' See the important studies of Tessa Watt: *Cheap Print*, and 'Piety in the pedlar's pack: continuity and change, 1578-1630' in Margaret Spufford, ed, *The World of Rural Dissenters, 1520-1725* (Cambridge University Press, Cambridge, 1995) pp.235-272.

[7] John White, *A Way to the Tree of Life. . . Directions for the Profitable Reading of the Scriptures* (London, 1647) p.341.

[8] R Ro[gers] et al, *A Garden of Spiritual Flowers* (London, 1632 ed) p.125: am pss.3, 5, 19; pm pss.4, 92. See also chapter 4 of this study.

[9] Malcolm Deacon, *Philip Doddridge of Northampton, 1702-1751* (Northamptonshire Libraries, Northampton, 1980) pp.105, 143.

[10] Orton, *Religious Exercises*, pp.221-2. John Mason, *The Lord's Day Evening Entertainment*, 4 vols (London, 1752).

Early in the nineteenth century prayers appropriate to the liturgical year were introduced into Congregational and Presbyterian family prayerbooks.[1] Hymns largely replaced psalms, and by late century might be said rather than sung. Presbyterian Alexander Fletcher and Congregationalist Charles Williams published what I term 'family breviaries'—volumes containing, in the same opening, a hymn, scripture reading plus brief commentary, and a comprehensive didactic prayer for every day of the calendar year.[2] These books enjoyed extensive circulation in Great Britain and its colonies, Ireland and North America. The convenient package was meant to entice heads of family to undertake family worship. But whether they were used or merely decorated parlour shelves is difficult to gauge: some surviving copies are in good condition, others, in tatters. Meal graces no longer appeared in English prayerbooks, and it is assumed that children offered simple rote prayers. By 1882 there is evidence of the 'juvenilization' of family worship: simple didactic services for Sunday evening pitched at the under-twelves.[3] Few family prayerbooks were published in England after the turn of the century; a corresponding decline in practice is probable.

From the Reformation in Scotland, church authorities expected all families to join in common prayers,[4] and periodically attempted to legislate the practice.[5] Sung metrical psalms,[6] a chapter of scripture with discussion or catechetical instruction,[7] plus the 'Forms of Prayer to be used in Private Houses' appended to the BCO[8] were customary into the mid-seventeenth century, after which extempore prayer in scriptural language was favored. This basic outline continued through the nineteenth century. From the mid-eighteenth century onwards, there was a slow decline in households worshiping together. In 1754, Samuel Davies observed both a general decay in 'practical religion' as well as a 'considerable number of pious people' in Edinburgh. And in 1822, Church of Scotland minister Thomas Wright (1785-1855) reluctantly acknowledged that most families were most likely to pray together on the Sabbath, if at all.[9]

Scots graces, if only over a simple meal of potatoes, oat cakes, butter and milk, tended to be long.[10] Free Church members preserve traditional practice: to this day they say grace before and *after* meals *and* at coffee/tea breaks.[11]

---

[1] William Jay, *The Domestic Minister's Assistant*, 2nd ed (Bath, 1820).

[2] A. Fletcher, *A Guide to Family Devotion* [1st ed 1834] new ed (London, [c 1865]). [C. Williams], J. Harris ed, et al, *The Altar of the Household* (London, 1853).

[3] Benjamin Waugh, *Sunday Evenings with my Children* (London, 1882).

[4] J. Knox, 'A Letter of Wholesome Counsel' (1556) in D. Laing, ed, *The Works of John Knox* (Edinburgh, 1855) vol 4, p.137. Dunlop, *op. cit.*, vol 2, pp.586-7.

[5] McMillan, *op. cit.*, pp.77-8. Dunlop, *op. cit.*, vol 1, pp.447-8, 458. Cf Boyd, *op. cit.*, pp.70-95.

[6] McMillan, *op. cit.*, pp.80-1: 'sang schules' were in all principal towns in the sixteenth century.

[7] 1647 'Directory for Family Worship' in Dunlop, *op. cit.*, vol 1, p.450.

[8] Sprott, *BCO*, pp.178-94. Scots also used English Puritan books: T. Erskine, ed, *Letters of the Rev. Samuel Rutherford*, 2nd ed (Glasgow, 1827) p.195.

[9] Pilcher, *op. cit.*, pp.99, 130. [Wright] *The Morning and Evening Sacrifice* (Edinburgh, 1823 edn.) p.194.

[10] Elizabeth S. Haldane, *The Scotland of our Fathers: A Study of Scottish Life in the Nineteenth Century* (Alexander Maclehose, London, 1933) pp.39-40. James Inglis, *Oor Ain Folk: Being Memories of Manse Life*, 3rd ed (Edinburgh, 1895) pp.39-40.

[11] *Ibid*, p.243. Telephone conversation with J. Christopher Ledgard, 9 July 1996.

Boyd suggests that the decline of family worship in the Victorian era was due to the dwindling fortunes of middle-class families and Sunday school that supplanted parental religious responsibility for children.[1] A surge in publication of family prayerbooks during this time[2] indicated interest in but also anxiety for the survival of family worship.

In seventeenth-century New England, Puritan families worshipped according to the guidelines of English devotional books such as Bayly's *The Practice of Piety* and *The Garden of Spiritual Flowers*.[3] New England Native Americans evangelized by John Eliot and others followed Puritan practice, observing family prayer morning and evening, 'and with more affection they crave God's blessing upon a little parched corn, and Indian stalks, than many of us do upon our greatest plenty.'[4] Inclusion of African slaves in family worship was a religious duty, but most likely to occur in deeply religious households, and where master/mistress and slave were close.[5]

Individualism, deism, rationalism, and the preoccupations of a fledgling nation all had a deleterious impact on family worship in the eighteenth century.[6] By 1787 sermons were most likely to be read or 'repeated' on Sunday evenings, and during the nineteenth century families were less likely to use psalms or hymns in family worship, or grace after meals.[7] In 1847 Presbyterian James Alexander acknowledged that family worship was widely disregarded for the 'secret dread of the sneer, even of a child or a servant.'[8]

McDannell noted an increased *interest* in domestic piety between 1830 and 1870, due to evangelical influence; at the same time, cultural changes were transforming family worship from a traditional ritual with father as priest to a didactic one with mother as teacher. By the turn of the century family evening worship was being replaced by the bedside prayer of children.[9]

Family worship continues to be practised among some families in the Reformed Church in America and the Christian Reformed Church in North America (particularly at mealtime) in the twentieth century, with other denominations interested in recovering the practice.[10]

---

[1] Boyd, *op. cit.*, p.93.

[2] John R. Macduff, *Family Prayers* (London, 1853) had a 31st ed in 1869; [Church of Scotland] *Prayers for Family Worship*, 1859 and subsequent eds and supplements.

[3] Hambrick-Stowe, *op. cit.*, 144-7.

[4] Thomas Shephard, *The Clear Sun-shine of the Gospel Breaking Forth Upon the Indians in New-England* (London, 1648) sig A7r, pp.5, 14-5. James P. Ronda and James Axtell, *Indian Missions: A Critical Bibliography* (Indiana University Press, Bloomington, 1978).

[5] John Robinson, *The Testimony and Practice of the Presbyterian Church in Reference to American Slavery* (Cincinnati, 1852) pp.38-9, 122-3, 126-7, 132-3, 140-3. Mary Beth Norton, '"My Resting Reaping Times": Sarah Osborn's Defense of Her "Unfeminine" Activities, 1767' in *Signs: Journal of Women in Culture and Society* 2 (1976) pp.515-529. [Mary Terhune] *op. cit.*, pp.98-100.

[6] McDannell, *op. cit.*, p.5.

[7] 'The Directory for Secret and Family Worship' in *A Draught of the Form and Discipline of the Presbyterian Church in the United States of America* (NY, 1787) pp.117-8. Alexander, *op. cit.*, p.218.

[8] *Ibid*, pp.246, 255.

[9] McDannell, *op. cit.*, pp.xv, 6-8, 93, 135, 152.

[10] Personal communication with Luella Karay, 1990, confirms church members of both denominations have home prayer in the Zeeland-Holland area of Michigan, USA. Her family [RCA] observed

[continued on p.37 opposite]

3. HUSBAND AND WIFE PRAYING TOGETHER

Common devotions of husband and wife were the 'family' prayer of childless or 'empty-nest' couples, but were also observed morning and evening, as by a distinct community and are attested in England, Scotland and North America.[1] Schücking suggests that part of the practice, termed 'humiliation' by Puritans, derived from medieval lay reciprocal confession.[2] J. H. Merle D'Aubigné, the French-Swiss Reformed historian, was aware of patristic precedent: Clement of Alexandria advised Christian spouses to pray and read the bible together daily, and Tertullian praised believers who prayed and fasted together.[3]

Shared devotions of husband and wife, considered a mutual duty[4] by English Puritans, were varied and informal, combining prayer, a review of the state of their souls and lives, and the reading of scripture or a devotional book.[5] The intimacy of the practice makes it difficult to ascertain its survival to the present day.[6]

4. INDIVIDUAL DEVOTION

Disciplines of individual devotion have been universal among the Reformed from earliest times through the nineteenth century. Calvin preached: 'we be commanded to pray every man by himself at home in his house, in his chamber, in his bed, and at his table. . . .'[7] Prayer, scripture reading, meditation, and self-examination were elements consistently

---

midday meal and supper with grace before and a chapter and long prayer with LP, after meal. They sang hymns at supper, and when snow precluded church attendance, their father read a sermon from a book [1930's-1940's]: Luella Meengs Karay, ed, *Stories for the Meengs Family*, (unpublished pamphlet, [Elkhart, IN], 1995) p.26. See also: Karay Tripp, 'Daily Prayer,' pp.211-2, note 93. Marjorie J. Thompson, *Family, The Forming Center: A Vision of the Role of the Family in Spiritual Formation* (Upper Room Books, Nashville, 1989).

See also: Gerstner, *op. cit.*, on the Dutch Reformed in the Netherlands and Colonial South Africa, pp.31-2, 43-5, passim; p.169 documents home worship among isolated Afrikaner farmers to the present. Szigeti, art cit, pp.133-5: Hungarian domestic worship and its debt to English Puritanism. Dennis McEldowney, *Presbyterians in Aotearoa 1840-1900* (The Presbyterian Church of New Zealand, np, 1990) pp.33, 49, 127. S. Raapoto, 'The Christian Family' in *Beyond the Reef: Records of the Conference of Churches and Missions in the Pacific* (International Missionary Council, London, 1961) pp.60, 65, documents family worship among Presbyterians in Tahiti c 1960.

[1] [O. Heywood] , *Narrative of the Holy Life and Happy Death of. . . John Angier* (London, 1683) p.41. Meikle, *op. cit.*, p.xxxv [Associate Synod], *Life of Ashbel Green*, p.148.

[2] Schücking, *op. cit.*, p.41; cf James 5.16.

[3] Baxter, CD, 2.7, pp.413-5. Henry, *Philip Henry* citing I Peter 3.7b (principal warrant).

[4] Turner, *op. cit.*, vol 1, p.329.

[5] 'Family Worship' from *Discourses and Essays* (Glasgow, 1846) pp.249-64: reprint ed: Presbyterian Heritage, Dallas, 1989 pp.7-8. No citations are given, but Tertullian reference is likely to be to *Ad Uxorem* 2. 5-6.

[6] Marlene de Groot Maggetti (raised CRCNA), letter of March 1990 to the author, discovered her parents' practice of informal morning prayers during a camping trip.

[7] *Calvin: Deuteronomie*, p.660.

used across centuries and national boundaries.[1] The devout commonly observed set hours at morning, noon and evening, for perhaps one-quarter to one-half an hour, while some prayed twice daily and others, more frequently.[2] Set hours were viewed as necessary but not sufficient to fulfill the command to pray without ceasing. Continuity in prayer was provided by two methods: a) prayer before distinct actions such as reading the Bible, mealtime and work,[3] and b) ejaculatory prayer, offered throughout the day.[4] Furthermore, into the nineteenth century, individuals observed 'secret' fast and thanksgiving days. Jesus' command to 'pray in secret,' Matt. 6.6 was the foundation of individual prayer. Reformed folk knew they did not pray in isolation but were in God's presence [coram Deo]; their prayers were in common with the church.[5]

In the sixteenth century individuals prefaced scripture reading with a prayer for illumination, a practice advocated by Calvin,[6] and followed it with meditation, both to absorb what was read and to prepare for prayer.[7] Prayer generally concluded with the Lord's Prayer and sometimes with the Apostles' Creed. Use of these two items, morning and evening, perpetuates an obligation already assumed by St Augustine's time to be

---

[1] 'Secret' prayer was taught to and practised by Native Americans, African-Americans and others evangelized by missionaries. eg: Experience Mayhew, *Indian Converts: Or, Some Account of the Lives and Dying Speeches of a Considerable Number of the Christianized Indians of Martha's Vineyard* (London, 1727) pp.176, 232, 236, 238. James P. Ronda, 'Generations of Faith: The Christian Indians of Martha's Vineyard' *William and Mary Quarterly*, 3rd Series, 38 (1981) p.389 asks whether Indians' prayer in secluded places represents a 'kind of Christian vision quest.' J. A. U. Gronniosaw, *A Narrative of the Most Remarkable Particulars in the Life of James Albert Ukawsaw Gronniosaw* (Bath, printed; Newport, RI, reprinted, 1774): James, b. c. 1714 in Africa was purchased as a slave by 'Rev. Freelandhouse' [probably T. J. Frelinghuysen, a Reformed minister] with whom he stayed about eighteen years. This minister taught him to pray (pp.18-9); Gronniosaw prayed three times daily in the woods and read Baxter (p.24). Freed about 1747, he accompanied G. Whitefield to England, for he wanted to see Baxter's parish, Kidderminster. Gronniosaw's description of his native religious practice: worship on Saturday at 3am until the sun was a certain height (10-11am), kneeling with hands help up, observing strict silence under a palm tree—raises the question of the synthesis of native and Reformed practice. John Williams, *A Narrative of Missionary Enterprises in the South Sea Islands* (NY, 1837) p.120, attests to private prayer as 'very general' among the people of the south Pacific Hervey Islands.

Calvin: Institutes 3.20.92, vol 2, p.892. Tho[mas] Sorocold, *Supplications of Saints* [1st ed 1608], 25th ed (London, 1639) provides prayers for morning, noon and evening. This work had forty-five eds by 1754.

[3] Col. 3.17 was the most common warrant. Drelincourt, *op. cit.*, pp.88, 112. *Calvin: Deuteronomie*, p.959: on prayer before work, citing Deut. 28.12.

[4] Warrants: I Chron. 5.20, Neh. 2.4; I Cor. 15.28. Doddridge, *op. cit.*, pp.185-6.

[5] *Calvin: Institutes* 3.20.38, vol 2, p.901; Baxter, CD, 3.10, pp.614ff.

[6] *Calvin: Deuteronomie*, p.404: 'as ofte as we come to any sermon, or read the holy scripture: let us pray to God to touch us inwardly and to make the doctrine available.'

[7] *Maister Beza's Hovshold Prayers*, 1607 ed, sig B8ᵛ. Meditation, a complex subject, cannot be discussed here in detail. For the Reformed, its use as sermon technique adapted to the individual eventually overrode its contemplative functions. Scripture reading was central to Reformed devotion. On literacy, see: *The Oxford Encyclopedia of the Reformation*, sv 'Literacy' by R. A. Houston, vol 2, pp.429-434. David D. Hall, *Worlds of Wonder, Days of Judgment: Popular Religious Belief in Early New England* (Alfred A. Knopf, NY, 1989) pp.21-70.

binding on the baptized.[1] Individuals sang psalms during private devotion.[2] Self-examination was used to prepare for worthy reception of the Lord's Supper as well as for penitential prayer.[3] On Saturday evening or early Sunday morning individuals prepared for public assembly in their devotions, and pastors advised them to record the chief points of sermons for meditation.[4]

In the seventeenth century, in addition to praying morning, noon and evening, people prayed and/or meditated immediately upon waking and as they drifted to sleep, beginning and ending the day 'in him who is both first and last.'[5] When alone, French Reformed pastor Charles Drelincourt (1595-1669) fell on his knees to pray whenever he heard the clock strike the hour. This temporal *memento mori* was also practised by Roman Catholics.[6]

Scripture reading (the Old Testament, morning; New Testament, evening)[7] was often supplemented with commentaries and other 'godly' authors.[8] While the concluding Lord's Prayer persisted, the Creed generally fell out of private use. Private psalm-singing, in course or selective, continued in this century.[9] Self-examination was used in the evening: one gave an account of one's day to God before praying for forgiveness and amendment of life. Devotions might conclude with the Grace ('with me').[10] By the second half of the seventeenth century, renewal of the baptismal covenant was recommended on a regular basis.[11]

In the eighteenth century less is said of prayer at noon and of prayer or meditation upon waking or just before sleep, although Doddridge still recommended the latter.[12] Psalmody or hymns were considered a normal part of secret devotion and were to be sung aloud in a

---

[1] J. A. Jungman, *Pastoral Liturgy*, tr R. Walls (Challoner, London, 1962) p.198. Among Puritans, 'O Lord, increase our faith,' was a cue for the Creed. (The author is grateful to D. H. Tripp for discovering this link). Sometimes the Creed was dispensed with and only the cue retained: cf Norden, *Pensive Mans Practice*, who appends the tag to most prayers.

[2] French Reformed martyr Phillipine De Luns (d 1558) was often heard singing psalms 25 and 42 in prison: James I. Good, *Women of the Reformed Church* (np, 1901) p.96. *James Melville*, p.126: The 1584 Order there mentioned exhorts individuals to 'private exercise' for which a Bible and psalmbook were necessary.

[3] Calvin, 'Short Treatise on the Holy Supper of our Lord Jesus Christ' in *Tracts containing Treatises...*, tr H. Beveridge (Edinburgh, 1849) vol 2, p.175. David Foxgrover, 'Self-Examination in John Calvin and William Ames,' in W. Fred Graham, ed, *Later Calvinism: International Perspectives*, C. G. Nauert, Jr, Gen Ed, Sixteenth Century Essays & Studies, vol XXII (Sixteenth Century Journal Pub, Kirksville, Missouri, 1994) pp.451-469.

[4] *Works of Henry Smith*, vol 1, pp.396-7, 317-37.

[5] Joceline, *op. cit.*, pp.13-15, 77, a practice encouraged by Calvin: *Calvin: Deuteronomie*, p.473

[6] D'Assigny, Preface to Drelincourt, *op. cit.*, sig A2ᵛ. cf C. Mather, *The Thoughts of a Dying Man* (Boston, 1677) pp.38-9. Jesuit [Hieremias Drexelius], *The Angel Gvardians Clock* (Rouen [c 1630]) p.14, citing John 11.9.

[7] Bayly, *Practice of Piety*, 1640 ed, p.213 advises three chapters a day.

[8] *Garden of Spiritual Flowers*, pp.122-3. G. Diodati, *Pious Annotations Vpon the Holy Bible*, tr R. B. (London, 1643).

[9] The lack of harmony in church singing among the Dutch Reformed in the seventeenth-century was explained as due to the fact that 'many people sang psalms at home while working, and preferred their own variations...' Van Deursen, *op. cit.*, p.270, citing C. Huygens, *Ghebruick en ongbebruick van 't orgel in de kerken der Vereenighde Nederlanden*, 2nd ed (Amsterdam, 1659) p.113.

[10] *Garden of Spiritual Flowers*, pp.24, 109-10; Bayly, *op. cit.*, p.287.

[11] Baxter, CD, 3.3, pp.559-60.

[12] Doddridge, *op. cit.*, pp.179, 189.

low voice. Henry Grove stated that Ps 19 was the morning psalm and Ps 8 the evening one.[1] Covenant renewal continued to be important.[2]

During the nineteenth century the traditional practice of secret worship gradually eroded.[3] Beginning at the turn of the twentieth century several suggestions for a renewed personal office were published.[4]

Eucharistic piety, central to Reformed private devotion from an early date, was at its richest in the seventeenth and eighteenth centuries. On the evening before or morning of the sacrament, individuals prepared by self-examination and prayer. During the sacrament they renewed their baptismal covenant, offering themselves completely to God as they meditated vividly on the crucified Savior. As they saw others receive bread and wine, they prayed for them and for the whole Body of Christ, the church, looking forward in hope to the eternal supper of the Lamb. Returning home, they engaged in further prayer and self-examination. A variety of communion manuals were used—sacramental theology, sermons and prayerbooks.[5]

---

[1] Bennet, *Christian Oratory*, pp.626-3 citing Acts 16.25. H. Grove, *A Discourse of Secret Prayer* (London, 1726) p.56. However the 'Directory for Worship' of the 1787 *Draft* of the PECUSA did not list psalms or hymns as a secret worship duty.

[2] Bennet, *op. cit.*, pp.18-23, outlines 'secret worship duty': brief prayer for illumination, scripture plus commentary study, meditation, self-examination (daily), prayer (invocation, thanksgiving, confession, petition, intercession, self-dedication, all in the name and mediation of the Lord Jesus, 'Amen' and Lord's Prayer), psalmody.

[3] There were always exceptions: eg John Brown, *Rab and his Friends* (1906; reprint ed J. M. Dent, London, 1934) 'Jeems the Doorkeeper,' pp.112-124, a United Presbyterian layman who sang psalms using only seven tunes, one for each morning of the week, then, in the evening, the same tunes, in reversed order. Harbaugh, *Golden Censer*, p.16 still encouraged singing a hymn with one's prayers (1860).

[4] H. J. Wotherspoon, *Kyrie Eleison: A Manual of Private Prayers* (Edinburgh, 1899). G. S. Stewart, *The Lower Levels of Prayer* (SCM, London, 1939) pp.130-43.

[5] Holifield, *op. cit.*, Karay Tripp, 'Daily Prayer,' note 121, p.216. Schmidt, *op. cit.*, pp.115-168.

8. Conclusions

Through the centuries, Reformed folk have prayed in cathedrals, town and rural churches, under palm, banyan and oak trees, on horseback, while working, in bed, as they laboured to give birth and on their deathbeds. They prayed everywhere and aimed to pray without ceasing. Subjected to persecution (white Americans excluded) they did not give up on God when driven from common prayers, but prayed all the harder, in caves, barns and homes. As opposition relented, they sought out both old and new ways of worshipping together.

They have been stereotyped by themselves and other communions as disembodied, a-sacramental, antiliturgical, following an individualistic creed. Their heritage, wrapped under a blanket of spiritual and historical amnesia, is quite the reverse: a people who prayed with their bodies as well as mind and soul, who knelt, prostrated themselves, beat their breast, lifted hands and eyes, wept for their sins and wept in gratitude; who recalled their baptism and its implications on a frequent basis, studied sacramental theology and prepared for reverent reception of the eucharist; who drew neighbours into their homes to pray, joined townspeople in prayer meetings and common prayers, prayed at home and with those who worked for and with them, and in the triune community of God's presence; a people devoted to intercession, alms-giving, to all manner of charity and kindness, seeking 'the welfare of the Body.'[1]

'The Reformed Tradition' shows remarkable consistency across centuries and national boundaries, but the Genevan-Scots-Puritan heritage is not representative of the tradition as a whole, in many respects. A richer, nuanced understanding is required. The seventeenth-century English Puritan listening to a sermon with his hat on is Reformed, but so is the Lithuanian woman making a curtsy at the name of Jesus. The music-less word-centred services of early Zurich are Reformed; so too are the non-preaching services of Hessen with choir, organ and other instruments.

Nowhere has the Genevan-Scots-Puritan stereotype done more harm than in assumptions regarding the liturgical year. Admittedly, New England Puritans observed market hours on Christmas and Easter, but their Dutch neighbours a little to the south [New Amsterdam] observed the major feasts, administering the Lord's Supper on Easter, Pentecost and Christmas, where possible, and closing shop doors not only on Christmas, for example, but for eight days following; and during the same time-frame, Lithuanian and Polish Reformed celebrated feasts of the Virgin Mary and the days and hours of the Passion. Eastern-European Reformed church traditions are much neglected. The western-European Reformed year has also been overshadowed.[2]

---

[1] Bennet, *Second Part*, p.141, from sermon 'Of the Unity of the Church' [text: I Cor. 12.13].

[2] Daniel James Meeter, *The 'North American Liturgy': A critical edition of the Liturgy of the Reformed Dutch Church in America, 1793*, PhD dissertation, Drew University, 1989 (University Microfilms International, Ann Arbor, Mich, 1990) pp.8, 58, 73. Singleton, *op. cit.*, p.301. Howard G. Hageman, 'Some Notes on the Use of the Lectionary in the Reformed Tradition,' in J. E. Booty, ed, *The Divine Drama in History and Liturgy: Essays presented to Horton Davies*, D. Y. Hadidian, Gen Ed, Pittsburgh Theological Monographs, New Series, 10 (Pickwick Publications, Allison Park, 1984) pp.163-178. And see German Reformed Church provisions for the liturgical year in: *An Order of Worship for The Reformed Church*, 5th ed (Phil, 1869), Harbaugh, *Golden Censer*, pp.235-250.

In general, in addition to the five major feasts, the Reformed sought a return to a primitive celebration of liturgical time. The summit was the Lord's Day, celebrated as weekly Pasch: the day of resurrection, the ascension, and the out-pouring of the Holy Spirit; also, the day of assembly and the day of communion, the first day of creation and harbinger of the everlasting day, the day of rest. The memory of Christ's resurrection is dominant.[1] Even the cycle of night and day was paschal: Reformed folk went to bed as to the grave, commending themselves into God's hands, as Jesus entrusted himself to the Father on the cross (Luke 23.46), and woke from sleep, resurrected, greeting the risen Sun of righteousness in their first thoughts and prayers.[2]

The relationship of Reformed daily prayer to pre-Reformation tradition is complex. Important strands of continuity with late medieval practice have been and will continue to be uncovered. Many elements of Reformed devotion attributed to Puritans, were approved, in fact, by Calvin and other Reformers, who may well be passing on pre-Reformation practice or slightly reworking it. When they overturned the tables, they looked to scripture and the early church for a vision of how Christian people could pray without ceasing in the workday world. Patristic connections and warrants, in Latin, Greek or English, fill the margins of Reformed treatises. A few of those warrants have been discussed here, but it would be a service if a specialized study of the matter were made.[3] Why does the patristic pattern of a word-centred service on the penitential days of Wednesday and Friday recur among the Reformed in the Electoral Palatinate, Hessen, Hungary, Scotland and elsewhere?[4] Is this an accident of history or a conscious choice for continuity? Or both?

The pattern of gradual disintegration observed in family and private worship illustrates Baumstark's second law of liturgical law of evolution, that change is resisted at the more solemn seasons.[5] In the case of the Reformed, practices that are disappearing are preserved on, and reserved to, Sunday. Reformed daily prayer must be considered a liturgical tradition.[6] The European Reformers instituted public daily prayer wherever feasible, and these services continued, in some cases, to the present day. They also commended prayer at set hours by families and individuals. The content of secret and family prayer strongly correlates with public liturgy. All prayer was consciously in union with the wider church, and adherence to biblical hours meant that people were praying at roughly the same times. The strong baptismal and eucharistic dimensions of Reformed devotion, including covenant renewal—which combines baptismal and eucharistic import—underscore its liturgical character.[7]

---

[1] Baxter, CD, 2.18, pp.446-7. Orton, *Religious Exercises*, pp.174ff.

[2] Hambrick-Stowe, *op. cit.*, pp.147-9.

[3] Cf Balthasar Fischer, 'The Common Prayer of Congregation and Family in The Ancient Church' *Studia Liturgica* 10 (1974) pp.106-124. Fischer, p.123, notes that Chrysostom often exhorted scripture reading in the family but met with some resistance— 'their bishop is trying to turn them into monks.'

[4] A-G. Martimort, ed, *The Church at Prayer Vol 4: The Liturgy and Time* (Liturgical Press, Collegeville, Minn, 1986) p.26. See McMillan, *op. cit.*, p.147 on Wed and Fri preaching and 'fish' days.

[5] A. Baumstark, *Comparative Liturgy*, tr F. L. Cross, (Mowbray, London, 1958) p.27.

[6] I refer to Paul Bradshaw's understanding of 'liturgical': *art cit*, (*Worship*) p.10.

[7] See prayerbook bibliography in Karay Tripp, 'Daily Prayer,' pp.218-219.

THE GROUP FOR RENEWAL OF WORSHIP (GROW)

This group, originally founded in 1961, has for well over twenty years taken responsibility for the Grove Books publications on liturgy and worship. Its membership and broad aims reflect a highly reforming, pastoral and missionary interest in worship. Beginning with a youthful evangelical Anglican membership in the early 1970s, the Group has not only probed adventurously into the future of Anglican worship, but has also with growing sureness of touch taken its place in promoting weighty scholarship. Thus the list of 'Grove Liturgical Studies' (published on page 46 overleaf) shows how, over a twelve-year period, the quarterly Studies added steadily to the material available to students of patristic, reformation and modern scholarly issues in liturgy. In 1986 the Group was approached by the Alcuin Club Committee with a view to publishing the new series of Joint Liturgical Studies, and this series is, at the time of writing, in its tenth year of publication, sustaining the programme with three Studies each year.

Between the old Grove Liturgical Studies and the new Joint Liturgical Studies there is a large provision of both English language texts and other theological works on the patristic era. A detailed consolidated list is available from the publishers.

Since the early 1970s the Group has had Colin Buchanan as chairman and Trevor Lloyd as vice-chairman.

THE ALCUIN CLUB

The Alcuin Club exists to promote the study of Christian liturgy in general, and in particular the liturgies of the Anglican Communion. Since its foundation in 1897 it has published over 130 books and pamphlets. Members of the Club receive some publications of the current year free and others at a reduced rate.

Information concerning the annual subscription, applications for membership and lists of publications is obtainable from the Treasurer, The Revd. T. R. Barker, 11 Abbey Street, Chester CH1 2JE (Tel. 01244 347811, Fax. 01244 347823).

The Alcuin Club has a three-year arrangement with the Liturgical Press, Collegeville, whereby the old tradition of an annual Alcuin Club major scholarly study has been restored. The first title under this arrangement was published in early 1993: Alastair McGregor, *Fire and Light: The Symbolism of Fire and Light in the Holy Week Services.* The second was Martin Dudley, *The Collect in Anglican Liturgy;* the third is Gordon Jeanes, *The Day has Come! Easter and Baptism in Zeno of Verona.*

The Joint Liturgical Studies have been reduced to three per annum from 1992, and the Alcuin Club subscription now includes the annual publication (as above) and the three Joint Liturgical Studies (with an extra in 1994). The full list of Joint Liturgical Studies is printed opposite. All titles but no. 4 are in print.

Alcuin/GROW Joint Liturgical Studies

All cost £3.95 (US $8) in 1996

1987 TITLES

1. (LS 49) **Daily and Weekly Worship—from Jewish to Christian**
   by Roger Beckwith, Warden of Latimer House, Oxford
2. (LS 50) **The Canons of Hippolytus**
   edited by Paul Bradshaw, Professor of Liturgics, University of Notre Dame.
3. (LS 51) **Modern Anglican Ordination Rites** edited by Colin Buchanan, then Bishop of Aston
4. (LS 52) **Models of Liturgical Theology** by James Empereur, of the Jesuit School of Theology, Berkeley

1988 TITLES

5. (LS 53) **A Kingdom of Priests: Liturgical Formation of the Laity: The Brixen Essays**
   edited by Thomas Talley, Professor of Liturgics, General Theological Seminary, New York
6. (LS 54) **The Bishop in Liturgy: an Anglican Study** edited by Colin Buchanan, then Bishop of Aston
7. (LS 55) **Inculturation: the Eucharist in Africa**
   by Phillip Tovey, then research student, previously tutor in liturgy in Uganda
8. (LS 56) **Essays in Early Eastern Initiation**
   edited by Paul Bradshaw, Professor of Liturgics, University of Notre Dame

1989 TITLES

9. (LS 57) **The Liturgy of the Church in Jerusalem** by John Baldovin
10. (LS 58) **Adult Initiation** edited by Donald Withey
11. (LS 59) **'The Missing Oblation': The Contents of the earlyAntiochene Anaphota** by John Fenwick
12. (LS 60) **Calvin and Bullinger on the Lord's Supper** by Paul Rorem

1990 TITLES

13-14 (LS 61) **The Liturgical Portions of the Apostolic Constitutions: A Text for Students**
   edited by W. Jardine Grisbrooke (This double-size volume costs double price (i.e. £7.90 in 1996))
15 (LS 62) **Liturgical Inculturation in the Anglican Communion**
   edited by David Holeton, Professor of Liturgics, Trinity College, Toronto
16. (LS 63) **Cremation Today and Tomorrow** by Douglas Davies, University of Nottingham

1991 TITLES

17. (LS 64) **The Preaching Service—The Glory of the Methodists**
   by Adrian Burdon, Methodist Minister in Rochdale
18. (LS 65) **Irenacus of Lyon on Baptism and Eucharist**
   edited with Introduction, Translation and Commentary by David Power, Washington D.C.
19. (LS 66) **Testamentum Domini** edited by Grant Sperry-White, Department of Theology, Notre Dame
20. (LS 67) **The Origins of the Roman Rite** Edited by Gordon Jeanes, then Lecturer in Liturgy, University of Durham

1992 TITLES

21. **The Anglican Eucharist in New Zealand 1814-1989** by Bosco Peters, Christchurch, New Zealand
22-23 **Foundations of Christian Music: The Music of Pre-Constantinian Christianity**
   by Edward Foley, Capuchin Franciscan, Chicago (second double-sized volume at £7.90 in 1996)

1993 TITLES

24. **Liturgical Presidency** by Paul James
25. **The Sacramentary of Sarapion of Thmuis: A Text for Students**
   edited by Ric Lennard-Barrett, West Australia
26. **Communion Outside the Eucharist** by Phillip Tovey, Banbury, Oxon

1994 TITLES

27. **Revising the Eucharist: Groundwork for the Anglican Communion**
   edited by David Holeton, Dean of Trinity College, Toronto
28. **Anglican Liturgical Inculturation in Africa** edited by David Gitan, Bishop of Klrinyaga, Kenya
29-30. **On Baptismal Fonts: Ancient and Modern**
   by Anita Stauffer, Lutheran World Federation, Geneva (Double-sized volume at £7.90)

1995 TITLES

31. **The Comparative Liturgy of Anton Baumstark** by Fritz West
32. **Worship and Evangelism in Pre-Christendom** by Alan Kreider
33. **Liturgy in Early Christian Egypt** by Maxwell E. Johnson

1996 TITLES

34. **Welcoming the Baptized** by Timothy Turner
35. **Daily Prayer in the Reformed Tradition: An Initial Survey** by Diane Karay Tripp
36. **The Ritual Kiss in the Early Church** by Edward Phillips (December 1996)

Grove Liturgical Studies

This series began in March 1975, and was published quarterly until 1986. Each title has 32 or 40 pages. No's 1, 3-6, 9, 10, 16, 44 and 46 are out of print. Asterisked numbers have been reprinted. Prices in 1996. £2.75.